Praise for *Crafting C[…]*

"As a lifelong artist, I am intimately familiar with the [...] are available to us when we engage in creative acts. L[...] in my heart, mind, and body, I relish the opportunity to learn the way my artistic [...], techniques, and mediums can open up specific spiritual channels and encourage an array of mindful, prayerful practices. I look forward to adding *Crafting Calm* to my bookshelf and sharing it with my artistic and spiritual sisters."

—Christine Mason Miller, author of *Ordinary Sparkling Moments*

"During these tumultuous times, it is more important than ever to cultivate our calm. Maggie Oman Shannon's *Crafting Calm* is a balm of a book that teaches us this subtlest of lessons."

—Phil Cousineau, author of *The Painted Word*

"I still have pictures in my head of my mom sitting and knitting in the pre-television days of my youth. It was a peaceful scene, seeing her take a meditative moment out of her household responsibilities. Today, in our nonstop world of ever-present text messages and emails, it is nice to have a book like this to help us both quiet our minds and enrich our lives, as the simple art of knitting did for my mom. So put down your cell phone, pick up this wonderful book, and begin creating your own comforting handiwork from *Crafting Calm*."

—Allen Klein, author of *The Art of Living Joyfully*

"In *Crafting Calm*, Rev. Maggie Oman Shannon gently reminds us that we are, by our very nature, both spiritual and creative beings. She inspires us to create as forms of self-exploration and spiritual growth, and guides us through fun and illuminating projects. From anointing oils to visual journals and prayer paintings to messages in bottles, Oman Shannon shows us how crafting can be part of our spiritual journey and a powerful way to connect to our very essence—the creative spirit within all of us. This book will inspire, uplift, and illuminate your spiritual path—and you'll also discover how much fun you can have when creating from spirit."

—Polly Campbell, author of *Imperfect Spirituality*

"At a certain point, I realized my so-called smart phone was making me stupider! Not to mention it added to my already considerable anxiety with its constant alarms, bells, and reminders. Maggie Oman Shannon has provided me with a marvelous book of ideas to help me craft the crazy away and reclaim my tranquility."

—Reeda Joseph, author of *Girlfriends Are Lifesavers*

crafting calm

For Barbara —
Every blessing to you as you "craft
calm"!
　　　　　Love and blessings,
　　　　　　　Maggie ♡

crafting calm

projects *and* practices *for*
creativity *and*
contemplation

MAGGIE OMAN SHANNON

FOREWORD BY MARY ANNE RADMACHER

VIVA
EDITIONS

Published in the United States by Viva Editions, an imprint of Cleis Press, Inc., 2246 Sixth Street, Berkeley, California 94710.

Printed in the United States.
Cover design: Scott Idleman/Blink
Cover photograph: Southern Stock & Brand X Pictures
Text design: Frank Wiedemann
Illustrations: Krishna Bhat
First Edition.
10 9 8 7 6 5 4 3 2 1

Trade paper ISBN: 978-1-936740-40-6
E-book ISBN: 978-1-936740-46-8

Library of Congress Cataloging-in-Publication Data

Oman Shannon, Maggie, 1958-
 Crafting calm : projects and practices for creativity and contemplation / Maggie Oman Shannon. -- First edition.
    pages cm
 Includes index.
 ISBN 978-1-936740-40-6 (pbk. : alk. paper)
 1. Handicraft--Psychological aspects. 2. Handicraft--Religious aspects. 3. Rites and ceremonies. 4. Meditation. I. Title.
 TT149.O43 2013
 745.5--dc23
                              2012046465

Dedicated to the Creator...
and to the creative spirit in each of us

Table of Contents

"What is important for the person on the spiritual path…is to discover and honor the creative inspiration that is uniquely his or hers to express."

—FRANCES VAUGHAN

"God is constantly creating, in us, through us, with us, and to cocreate with God is our human calling."

—MADELEINE L'ENGLE

"We speak of the Creator, but we seldom see that word as another word for 'artist.' And yet, clearly, a great artist made the world. We, in turn, are creations of the Creator, and are meant to continue its creativity by being creative ourselves. It might be said that the act of making art is actually a form of prayer."

—JULIA CAMERON

Foreword

IT'S A DELIGHT BUT NO SURPRISE THAT MAGGIE OMAN SHANNON has served up this amazing "recipe book" integrating prayer and spiritual practice with craft. She's been guiding tender hearts to meaningful prayer and spiritual practices through her ministry and writings for years. Now she offers this inspiring synergy of intention, heart, and craft to promote not only beauty but profound meaning in the process of that creating, that *making*. Maggie identifies dozens of "ingredients" that are foundational to a practice of artful making that delivers clear and focused calm.

The idea of *making* is such a familiar concept we barely give it thought...

We *make* it if we try, we make our beds, we make batches of cookies. We just make the train on time. We make friends. We make ourselves and others happy. We make time for the things that matter most to us. We make the best of situations. We make dinner.

Crafting Calm surprised me by helping me reflect on my own path and how it is that I've come to craft things. Being a maker is built into my ancestry and likely my DNA. My given name has *maker* built right in. Radmacher. Wheel maker. My grandfather and his brother were both sons of a wheel maker. When the need for handcrafted wheels declined with the advent of motor cars, my grandfather used his skills to make other things. A church in Portland, Oregon had a pulpit that my grandfather made. My father worked at a production plant making machines that helped others build things.

I watched my mother...make a house, make all our clothes, make each and every gift for any occasion. She made meals, she made home decor.

Between my two parents I had a practical model for making just about anything that was needed.

Observation-making is part of most everyone's experience. It's easy, accessible, and familiar. Reach just a little bit away from "making" and you arrive at "crafting" and "creating." These two processes are less comfortable for people. Mention craft or art at a general meeting and you'll hear a lot of qualifying statements, like "I've not a creative bone in my body" or "I'm not artistic at all." Such comments are common and unfounded. There are myriad ways to be artful. To craft. To make. We get to transfer our capacity to craft in one way and apply it to a new way.

Creating a project map, outlining strategic actions, organizing a calendar for more than one person, creating a phone tree, crafting a holiday event, organizing, orchestrating, pulling together, planning, anticipating, and incorporating: These are all familiar skills in the process of crafting.

I am a professional artist. I create and design things: that's my professional venue. I am a personal crafter, too. I craft and create, just as my mother did, when I want something unique for a friend. I've observed that my best and most inventive work emerges when I am crafting something for some sweet purpose. A gift for a friend. A bit of encouragement for someone who's going through a tough time. Something to encourage myself. These projects have no commercial thought to them. I'm not going to submit them to a design review process or suggest they become a product on a shelf for thousands of people to buy. I am making only one. My intention while making it always has the thought of the person who will receive it crafted right into it.

There's the impulse for my craft. I want to make a gift for someone...or something of beauty, function, or whimsy for myself. The outcome of this exercise is multiplied.

Not only do I produce an object at the end of the matter—I have created a mental land-scape for myself that is filled with joy, encouragement, and…calm. Maggie invites you to consider all acts of creation an opportunity to deepen your unique spiritual practice.

My history supports the concept of crafting calm. On the most stressful, chaotic days in my childhood home someone was bound to ask, "Where's mother?" The answer? Always, "She's making something in her craft room." Had Maggie's book been available to my family then, the answer would have more accurately been, "She's crafting calm."

When the intention is to bless, to gift, to explore, to discover…the thing which is *made* gives twice: once in the completion of its purpose or function, and again in the benefit of focused calm. Even when I'm learning a new craft, and enjoy the unnerving reality of having no real idea what I'm doing, there is calm in the process. It's accurate to say that when I make a gift…its first gift is given to me!

In *Crafting Calm,* Maggie offers a practical resource for pursuing the making of things… even if you are one of those who assert you "aren't that creative." This book is an ideal gift if you have friends who are often heard saying such silly things. It is both a rich inspira-tion and an invitation that is difficult to resist. Personally, this book called me to a deeper practice of giving as gifts things that I make. I know the time and purpose that I fold into the gift means so much to the receiver. We said it with pride as children, "Here, I made this for you." Maggie, with wonder and encouragement, calls her readers to engage in that process again. Maggie supports all the prompts that bring faithful souls to the table: an act of worship, service, or exploration; an expression of joy, sympathy, or encouragement.

The act of creation is rooted in the context of our spiritual being. Explore these pages—they will enlighten, inspire, and encourage your practice of crafting. Maggie helps expand ideas of what it is to be meditative, to be prayerful. She will spark ideas that are unique to you. The practical possibilities outlined in this book are just a beginning point. You'll begin by being drawn in by one of these awesome processes...and you'll be rewarded with that double gift.

Crafting. Creating. Making. In the action of manifesting something physical from something ineffable, we mirror the act of Great Creating. We call up, wake up a practice within ourselves that is ancient, almost mystical. The impulse to make fire, friends, goodness...all weave into the action of crafting. This book is a door through which you may walk and begin to see things differently. Go ahead. Maggie's been opening creative doors as a spiritual guide for years. Open the book, be inspired beyond your own expectations, and let Maggie and her many creative friends assure you that "you can make it." At every level. This book strengthened my own sense of the spiritual in the art of crafting. I trust it will strengthen your being as well.

Mary Anne Radmacher

Introduction

"Unless we are creators, we are not fully alive."
—MADELEINE L'ENGLE

IT IS A RARE DAY WHEN I HAVE NOTHING SCHEDULED, AND today I am supposed to be writing this book. Yet, looking around my office, I find myself distracted…my environment is not pristine, minimal, or clutter-free; instead, it is full of things that delight me visually or that I "might want someday" to use in a craft. There is a big plastic bin full of crafting possibilities that I am not sure where to store; clutter experts would tell me to chuck it all, or at the very least set a timer and choose the ten, maybe just five, things I can't live without.

But I open the lid and I see a myriad of possibilities: panels for the small glass terrarium shaped like a greenhouse, which I bought because it reminded me of the Glass Chapel I visualize in my mind during guided meditations; empty cigar boxes, both heavy cardboard and wooden, that

"The role of the artist I now understand as that of revealing through the world-surfaces the implicit forms of the soul…"
—JOSEPH CAMPBELL

will make perfect little shrines some Day-of-the-Dead weekend; a heart-shaped cardboard candy box, which could be used as the frame of an assemblage of things that I love.

There's the rub, for me—I see creative and spiritual possibilities in so much of what others would quickly cast off. It is a part of my brain that I don't seem able to shut off… wherever I go, whatever I look at, there is a part of me, a filter, that discerns whether or not it could be used for crafting—spiritually oriented crafting.

My nine-year-old daughter has inherited this sorting mechanism, and, if anything, hers is even stronger. She gladly squirrels away toilet-tissue tubes, bits of ribbon, pebbles, and more, certain that they all someday will be the perfect ingredients of "a craft." Once, in early December, she started constructing a small theater out of cardboard boxes, completely losing herself in the task. When asked a few days later what she wanted for Christmas, she responded—quite sincerely—that she would like more cardboard. That's my girl!

Looking at her creations, and contrasting them with mine, one might say that the craft activities that draw me are more spiritual in nature: They include a conscious intent to reflect in some way—or to be a vehicle for communing with—the Divine. But, though it may not be conscious, I also see a spiritual component threaded through my daughter Chloe's craft efforts—a desire to create something that didn't exist before, an attempt to engage the elements of life a little more deeply, an abandon into the creative space known as *kairos* time, the ethers where time stops and we enter into the state called flow.

I was an adult in my forties before I realized that the way I looked at things—this filter of mine that would analyze objects as potential elements in a spiritual craft—was not something shared by everyone. I was in a session with my spiritual director, telling her about a session that I had had earlier that month with a woman who was seeing me as her spiritual director. In that session, my spiritual directee had described noticing things around her—bits of dandelion fluff, beach glass, a small blue feather—as "Divine residue." I was captivated with this concept and it lingered in my mind for several days. That week, in a drugstore, looking at the "everything's a dollar" bin, I saw a number of tiny, plastic trashcans, not even a foot tall. I thought to myself, "What would someone *do* with those things?" and then it hit me—Divine residue! They would make perfect containers for Divine residue—and using one for that purpose would make me more mindful of noticing delightful bits of the Divine all around me.

Describing this to my spiritual director, she said something to me that in some ways changed my life, or at the least the way I view myself. She said, "You have a gift for seeing ways to create spiritual practices out of ordinary things." It hadn't ever occurred to me that I did...but once that comment registered, it was like throwing a pebble into a deep well, causing a ring of resonant ripples. *Yes,* came the inner response. With a deep, intuitive knowing, I realized that *this* is what I was doing, every time I saved a cigar box or bit of ribbon or an interesting stamp from a letter; I was gathering the supplies to turn my crafting into a spiritual practice. If you have read this far, then I imagine that you, too, have already embarked down this path or have a hunger to do so, which affirms you as being one of our tribe.

> "The eye is an organ of the soul; talking about creativity is talking about wholeness and cosmos and deep ecology and creation spirituality and our personal offering to the communion of the world."
>
> —M. C. RICHARDS

As I survey the objects around me, I note the ones that I just haven't been able to part with, no matter how old they are. There is a shrine I made from a Mexican tin container in shades of cobalt and yellow; it is titled "A Model of Energy as Exemplified by the 1994 Films of Keanu Reeves," and is adorned at the bottom with a photo of the muscled actor running in *Speed* and topped with a photo of the same actor in *Little Buddha*, considerably more slender and softer in appearance. I remember being intrigued at the time that these two film roles, released in the same year, demonstrated the span of the chakras, from root to crown—and I made the shrine as a meditation on how one person could embody all of those energies (not to mention that a photograph of Keanu is pretty easy on the eyes). I have a "Spirit House," a house-shaped box with divided sections in which I illustrated the various aspects of my life with paper images and dollhouse miniatures and a plastic bead that reads "God," placed at the highest point of the roof. And you will read of others that I've saved throughout this book—whose intent is to give you ideas and inspiration for making your own.

In the last decade or so, I've facilitated workshops to help people—primarily women—tap into that deep well in themselves, where the waters of creativity, spirituality, and personal identity blend and swirl. I've led people through making prayer beads and prayer journals, love boxes and collage triptychs, pastel mandalas and tiny tin shrines, and more. With time, and with the experience of not only my own immersion into a sacred, deeply satisfying, mystical place when creating, but also facilitating and being witness to others', I know that crafting can be a vehicle into the eternal. Would "A Model of Energy as Exemplified by the 1994 Films of Keanu Reeves" be classified as great art? No. Would it be something that someone else would want to buy, classifying it as sellable craft? Maybe, maybe not. Yet did it serve as a point of spiritual reflection around which I have revolved, not only in the making of it, but still in the viewing of it almost twenty years later? Most definitely, yes. And therein lies its intrinsic value.

As Marjory Zoet Bankson reminds us in her book *The Soulwork of Clay: A Hands-on Approach to Spirituality,* "According to the Oxford English Dictionary, the original meaning of *craft* is 'strength,' 'force,' 'power,' and 'virtue.' In German and Swedish, *kraft* moves beyond 'strength' into 'force of character.' In Dutch, *kracht* implies 'vigor' and 'potency.' It is only in English that there is the association of 'craft' with 'skill.' What if we were to shift our view of 'craft' from being a skill for a few to being a sign of the inner life force in each of us?" What if we were to shift this view, indeed?

And there's another view that may need shifting: the distinction between art and craft, which is somewhat insidious. For drawing a distinction between art and craft has created a divide: between the "haves" (of talent) and the "have-nots," between the trained and the untrained, and often between men (who have more often been considered by society to be the artists) and women (who have more often been considered by society to be the craftspeople). Working on this book, whose working subtitle was "Crafting as a Spiritual Practice," I asked people what distinction they made between art and craft, if any at all. For some, "craft" was a verb, not a noun—it was the methodology or techniques by which the final product, art, was made. For others it was a useless and elitist distinction—one that hearkened back to high school, where the "in" crowd (the artists) snubbed the less cool kids (the crafters).

There are many interesting examinations of this topic, and those who wish to explore it further have plenty of vehicles for doing so. For the purposes of this book, however, I use the words "art" and "craft" interchangeably, and sometimes abandon both in favor of the word "creation." The intention of this book is to help people with *process*—the spiritual journey of creating—rather than with the product or end result. When it comes to creating as a spiritual practice, form definitely follows function.

Because in the end the distinction between "art" and "craft" is an intellectual one, not a soulful one. The soulful statement that I hope this book makes is that whether you call yourself an artist or a craftsperson, both or neither, we are all creative. We are all creators. We are all creations of a Creator. It is to this that this book speaks—how we can stoke our deepest sense of ourselves and the Divine by employing the inherent flame that lies deep within each of us: creativity.

For that reason, too, this is not a highly technical "how-to" book. To focus on the "how-tos" would be antithetical to the larger point—that through art- and craft-making, we can commune with the Divine. Here you will find suggestions for beginning the journey, but it is assumed that once you find a particular craft that you resonate with and that is powerful to you personally in practicing the presence of God, you will go in search of more and better techniques to do that. You will be given some signposts for these explorations within the text (look for the "Guides for the Path" sections and in the Resource Section that concludes this book).

So I return to surveying my home office, and realize that this inner prompting to create in the presence of my Creator is why I will never be a minimalist...because I see new worlds, new creative and spiritual worlds, in the detritus of life. And I don't think it's too much of a stretch to look at this metaphorically: Dismantling things, saving certain elements of them, to be used again creatively...isn't that what we do—or should do—while going through life? It's what I've always loved about collage and assemblage—the idea that things that previously had no relationship to one another now do; that out of chaos or just plain randomness can come beauty; that we can consciously create something new and something beautiful out of *everything* in our lives.

This propensity to collect the debris of life was reaffirmed when I ran across this quotation from the late artist Corita Kent: "Artists, poets—whatever you want to call those people whose job is 'making'—take in the commonplace and are forever recognizing it as worthwhile. I think I am always collecting in a way—walking down a street with my eyes open, looking through a magazine, viewing a movie, visiting a museum or grocery store. Some of the things I collect are tangible and mount into piles of many layers, and when the time comes to use saved images, I dig like an archeologist through my lists and all the piles that have accumulated, and sometimes I find what I want and sometimes I don't."

And just as my spiritual director's comment created a seismic shift in my self-identity when she acknowledged my gift for creating spiritual practices from the ingredients of everyday life, so too has writing this book. When I look around my home office now, I see the impulses of my heart and hands, and my mind and soul, as writer, teacher, minister, and maker of crafts, if not "art." Just as I have difficulty getting rid of my breath-mint tins (they make great portable shrines!), I keep other resources around me, too—spiritual books, magazine images, ritual items, art supplies. But now I see them as being of a piece: all of them ingredients for navigating this life as a spiritual being having a human experience.

But I do want to underscore that the purpose behind the collection of these things is deeper than acquisition—this is not about collecting stuff (or making stuff) for stuff's sake. Just as a plane ticket does not represent the actual journey, our crafts—when made as a spiritual practice—do not represent the ultimate focus. They are simply the result of a spiritual process we undertake when we consciously decide to use our creating time as

"It is the creative potential itself in human beings that is the image of God."

—MARY DALY

an opportunity to be with our God.

This book is organized into eight chapters that speak to different intentions one can hold when approaching creating: crafting for calm, clarity, comfort, contemplation, creation, community, connection with others, and connection with Spirit. As you read through the different practices—there are five in each chapter, for a total of forty—you will no doubt note that potentially every craft holds the promise of calming, comforting, offering clarity, invoking contemplation, being a creation, and engendering community and connection with Spirit and others. Yet some activities will lend themselves more to a particular inner focus, and that is what these chapters will explore. The examinations of each craft also include a series of questions for journaling and reflection; as you contemplate these questions, your spiritual practice has already begun.

You'll also find lists of resources specific to certain crafts (look for the boxes marked "Guides for the Path"), suggestions for how to give your crafting a spiritual focus ("Crafting a Spiritual Practice"), quick ideas for particular projects ("Flashes of Inspiration"), and—sprinkled throughout—real-life accounts of crafters explaining in their own words how an artistic endeavor became something more, something sacred.

At first glance, some of these crafts and suggested spiritual practices might seem simple, even simplistic. But everything—including the simple act of breathing—always offers an invitation to go deeper. The key, the alchemical ingredient that changes an activity from craft to spiritual craft, is one's intention. How one consciously chooses to dedicate his or her creative time—and to what or whom one dedicates that creative time—is what turns an ordinary crafting experience into an experience of the holy.

Throughout the creation—the crafting—of this book, I've thought of it as a potpourri—a crystal container offering colorful seeds and blooms through which you can sift until you find the piece that captures your imagination. May this book be a starting point for you, or—if you've been crafting as a spiritual practice already—may it provide some fragrant reminders and inspirations for how to more fully integrate your spirituality with your creativity.

> "Creative soul qualities are…not just in the expression of creativity, but in the appreciation of it as well. Creativity is interactive and art is alchemical; its power is in its capacity to affect and transform the artist and the audience."
>
> –JEAN SHINODA BOLEN

As I was completing this book, I came across a wonderful quotation by the twentieth-century dance pioneer Isadora Duncan: "There are three kinds of dancers," she stated. "Those for whom dancing is physical exercise, those who dance to express emotion, and those who hand over their bodies to the inspiration of the 'soul.'" So, too, might there be three kinds of crafters—those for whom crafting is a creative exercise, those who craft to express emotion, and those who hand over their creations to the inspiration of the soul. It is my prayer that this book will inspire its readers to become members of that last group, those who hand over their craft to the inspiration of the soul.

Maggie Oman Shannon
San Francisco, California

CRAFTING FOR CALM

Chapter 1:

CRAFTING FOR CALM

"I feel that art has something to do with the achievement of stillness in the midst of chaos. A stillness which characterizes prayer, too, and the eye of the storm. I think that art has something to do with the arrest of attention in the midst of distraction."
—SAUL BELLOW

IN THIS WIRED, WILD WORLD, IT IS HARDER THAN EVER TO truly calm oneself—everywhere we go, we are assaulted by noise, stimulation, the never-ending crawl at the bottom of our television screens. As a recent *Washington Post* article explored, we are so caught up in our busy little worlds that sources of true beauty have trouble penetrating our rushed routines; how else to explain the fact that during a disheartening social experiment, in which world-class violinist Joshua Bell played unannounced and anonymously in a D.C. Metro station, hardly anyone (except children) bothered to stop and listen—and the collection for the renowned musician playing an hour-and-a-half in the subway was a mere thirty-two dollars?

The twentieth-century Catholic priest and writer Henri Nouwen once wrote that "Through the spiritual life we gradually move from the house of fear to the house of love" and the same thing

"A craft can only have meaning when it serves a spiritual way."
—TITUS BURKHARDT

could be said about the creative life. By immersing ourselves in our creative activity, we can still those voices around us and in us—we can enter the stillness that characterizes prayer and the "house of love." We can open ourselves and experience spaciousness.

Many, if not all of us, will find ourselves naturally calming or "gentling" down when we carve out the space to simply be with our Creator and our crafting materials. We will find, as the artist Corita Kent wrote, "there is an energy in the creative process that belongs in the league of those energies which can uplift, unify, and harmonize all of us."

Some crafts themselves are inherently calming; both the process and the product serve as vehicles for calm and even prayer. As Susan Gordon Lydon reminds us in *The Knitting Sutra*, "Handcrafts throughout history have often been fashioned with the aid of prayer, one prayer for each bead or each stitch, while keeping good thoughts to enhance the spiritual purpose of the object."

The practices in this chapter offer a spectrum of sensory appeal. From the smells and touch of anointing oils, to the sounds and sight of a tabletop meditation fountain, you will find activities here to truly help you to be still, and know that God is God.

ANOINTING OILS

Anoint—even the word itself sounds soothing, conjuring a succession of sensory associations: the fragrant scents, the soft stroke, the deep feeling that one is honored.

From Latin and French roots meaning "to smear," the act of anointing—of smearing or sprinkling a substance onto the skin—is done in most faith traditions around the world, using substances ranging from ashes to oil, water to clay.

My first experience with the transporting qualities of anointing oils came on one of my birthdays, when I gave myself the gift of an Ayurvedic massage called the Shirodhara at Deepak Chopra's spa near San Diego. Its highlight was the stream of warm oil that anointed the center of my forehead, my "third eye" or, as the spa materials define it, the intuitive energetic center. Billed as calming the central nervous system and integrating the mind and body, the massage felt far more profound—there is a transcendent quality to having oil rubbed on one's skin that feels deeply and divinely honoring.

> "Whatever you do, do it all for the glory of God."
>
> –1 CORINTHIANS 10:31

And personally using anointing oils—oils that have had essential oils added to them for fragrance and healing properties—can also be a powerful spiritual practice, as Ruah Bull, a spiritual director and coauthor of *Aromatherapy Anointing Oils: Spiritual Blessings, Ceremonies, and Affirmations*, describes: "I have been crafting with aromatherapy anointing oils since 1994, when I became interested in the psychological healing effects of essential oils. By 1996, as I started integrating it into my own daily self-care process, I began to experience the subtle and spiritual properties of the oils and how working with them was more profoundly a *spiritual* practice—both for me, and then eventually the people I shared it with.

"In 1996 I offered an eight-week program for women on the chakras, and decided to integrate aromatherapy anointing into the class," Ruah explains. "It quickly became apparent that this was more than even an 'energy' process, but was actually a sacred form of anointing, an ancient form of spiritual practice. After that class, evolving over the next few years, I began more consciously creating anointing oils for myself as part of my own prayer practice, and then began offering the process of creating and anointing with oils to spiritual directees who were wanting to develop personally meaningful ceremonies for themselves and friends and families. I also began to bring anointing oils into my other classes and workshops whenever we were going to be doing ceremony together."

Ruah's interest in anointing oils led her to co-write a book with Joni Keim Loughran, *Aromatherapy Anointing Oils.* As they write in their introduction, anointing oils can be used in a variety of settings, both individual and communal: "Aromatherapy anointing is a spiritual blessing given to another, a group, or to ourselves. It is not the source or essence of the blessing—it is merely a tool to help visualize, amplify, and manifest the intention of it. Aromatherapy anointing can be used for everyday occasions such as beginning the day, or for special occasions such as a graduation or birthday."

In the beloved and often memorized Psalm 23, the Psalmist praises God for the honor and blessings bestowed upon him—"You honor me by anointing my head with oil. My cup overflows with blessings" (New Living Translation). Integrating anointing oils into one's life can be a deeply honoring practice that reminds you (or the one anointed) of the blessings one has—including our own human body, one endowed with senses to appreciate the sight, smell, and touch of anointing oils.

Inner Inquiries for Journaling and Reflection

* How can I honor myself today?
* In what area of my life would I like to feel anointed ("to choose by or as if by Divine election")?

DIY: Crafting an Anointing Oil

For those who are interested in exploring the use of anointing oils as a spiritual practice, Ruah has generously created four different aromatherapy blends for the express purpose of enhancing and supporting creativity and spirituality:

Blend to Enhance and Support Creative Crafting
1 drop clary sage (or ylang ylang)
2 drops orange
1 drop jasmine
in 10 ml or 1 tablespoon of jojoba or organic vegetable oil

Two Blends to Support Meditation and Spiritual Practices

#1:

2 drops cedarwood (or sandalwood)

1 drop frankinscense

1 drop orange (or myrrh)

in 10 ml or 1 tablespoon jojoba or organic vegetable oil

#2:

5 drops lavender

5 drops frankinscense

in 10 ml or 1 tablespoon jojoba or organic vegetable oil

Blend to Set Sacred Space and Prepare for Crafting/Spiritual Practice

3 drops lavender

3 drops rose (or bergamot)

in 10 ml or 1 tablespoon jojoba or organic vegetable oil

Guides for the Path

The following resources may be helpful to you as you explore creating anointing oils as a spiritual practice:

Aromatherapy and Subtle Energy Techniques: Compassionate Healing with Essential Oils by Joni Keim Loughran and Ruah Bull (Frog, Ltd., 2000)

Aromatherapy Anointing Oils: Spiritual Blessings, Ceremonies, and Affirmations by Joni Keim Loughran and Ruah Bull (Frog, Ltd., 2001)

Daily Aromatherapy: Transforming the Seasons of Your Life with Essential Oils by Joni Keim Loughran and Ruah Bull (North Atlantic Books, 2008)

Subtle Aromatherapy by Patricia Davis (Random House UK, 2004)

Crafting a Spiritual Practice

"My best guidance is to take some time to *prepare*...enter into your craft as you would enter sacred space. Create some sort of ritual or prayer that marks your craft as spiritual practice–perhaps a body, mind, or heart process that sets an intention. That intention might be general, for example: 'May this craft time today bring me into alignment with the Creator of All. May my craft serve Love.' It might be specific to the moment–but I find being intentional about my craft as spiritual practice shifts my focus and consciousness so that body/mind/spirit comes into an alignment with my desire to serve and be an instrument for the Holy Spirit. And at the end of the craft/spiritual practice time, end with some sort of *closure* process–for me it's usually a prayer offering the time and craft to the Holy, but it could also be a ritual of some kind, even a special way of putting away and storing your craft items. My oils are in a special box, and I cover them with a beautiful cloth as I say my prayer. This beginning and ending with prayer/intention marks my craft for me as entering sacred time/space and practice."

–RUAH BULL

BIBLICAL GARDENS

Gardens are rich with fragrance and color and pattern, and a universal metaphor for the fecundity of life—and all of creation. Anyone who has ever spent enough time with a living plant to get dirt under her fingernails knows the spiritual joys—and lessons—that can be found in a garden.

Though I'm definitely a gardening novice, in my garden, I've discovered how quickly I'm able to lose the usual monkey-mind chatter and simply focus on the task at hand. Gardening is a wonderful practice for bringing one back into the present moment.

And, of course, gardens hold all kinds of metaphorical lessons: weeding the plot of land in my backyard, some undesired plants come up easily, some do not, and a few nasty roots have to be hacked away with all my tools at hand. So, too, is it with some of our less-helpful thoughts and habits—some we can dismiss quite easily, some require some work, and a few require every tool we have at hand and perhaps even getting some new tools to make real progress on the work.

> "Every art has its mystery, its spiritual rhythm."
>
> –D. T. SUZUKI

Both a craft that can promote calm as well as offer insight, gardening as a spiritual practice brings rich rewards, especially when the garden contains plants referenced in holy books or whose *raison d'etre* is for prayer. A number of people have created Biblical gardens, in which the plants included are referenced in the Scriptures.

However, when undertaking this, one does need to do so without getting overly attached to a perfect match—the nonattachment itself is a spiritual practice!—as different translations of the Scriptures make it hard to say with certainty exactly which plants were being refer- enced. And in that sense, the idea of crafting a Biblical or prayer garden becomes uniquely your own— which plants you choose should be meaningful to *you*.

Given that, there are still refer- ences to general categories of plants in the Old and New Testaments that you could explore including in your garden: vines and lilies, wheat and thistles, narcissus and mint, papyrus and olive. Find horticultural experts in your area who will help you to discern which plants will grow best in your garden. And if you live in a less hospitable climate for growing the above, consider creating a Biblical herb garden, which may grow best in a kitchen window. Once chosen, consider making labels for each plant, including a verse of Scripture in which that particular plant is named, to really make your gardening—whether indoor or outdoor—a "closer walk with God."

Whether we create a simple prayer garden, consciously choose outdoor plants that remind us of the ancient wisdom in the Scriptures, or work with herbs in a windowsill, we will be rewarded with nourishment from nature and the lessons nature can teach us. With mindfulness, we may find ourselves tending our lives like we tend our gardens— with diligence, with patience, and with joy in the process.

Inner Inquiries for Journaling and Reflection

* What are some of my favorite passages from the Bible (or any other holy book)? What are they saying to me about my life circumstances right now?

* What do particular scents—lavender, rose, peppermint—remind me of? What fragrances, or scents, do I need to surround myself with right now? What would calm me and why?

* What in my life feels sweet right now? Spicy? Energizing? Calming?

DIY: Crafting a Biblical Garden

If you choose to plant a garden with plants referenced in the Judeo-Christian scriptures, you might want to include some of the following:

Aloe ("Like valleys that stretch afar, like gardens beside a river, like aloes that the Lord has planted, like cedar trees beside the waters."—Numbers 24:6)

Coriander ("Now the house of Israel called its name manna; it was like coriander seed, white, and the taste of it was like wafers made from honey."—Exodus 16:31)

Cumin, Dill, and *Mint* ("Woe to you, scribes and Pharisees, hypocrites! For you tithe mint and dill and cumin, and have neglected the weightier matters of the law, justice and mercy and faith: these you ought to have done, without neglecting the others."—Matthew 23:23)

Mustard ("...the least of all seeds: but when it is grown, it is the greatest among herbs, and becometh a tree, so that the birds of the air come and lodge in the branches thereof."—Matthew 13:31)

Rose ("The wilderness and the dry land shall be glad, the desert shall rejoice and blossom; like the rose."—Isaiah 35:1)

"My God will always guide me,
Giving me relief in desert places.
My God will give a strength to my bones,
And I will be like a well-watered garden,
like a flowing spring whose waters never run dry."
—ISAIAH 58:11

Flashes of Inspiration

"One of the things I use in gardening is a 'muse-ical wand.' As an imaginative person, I need to stay in touch with my muse. I can call her to me anytime I am feeling blocked or uninspired with a very special tool that will draw my muse to me with sweet-smelling smoke. I keep a pot of the hardy and sun-loving herb sage on my windowsill, so it is handy all the time. To create the wand, I combine a long stalk of fennel with a twisted bundle of sage and long sticks of favorite incense, such as cinnamon or nag champa, my personal favorites. I braid the material tightly together into a wand using purple (for power) and gold (for money) string or thread. Before any artistic endeavor or meditation, I light one end of the wand with a candle and wave it around to clear my environment, allowing the smoke to clear out my mind in the process."

—BRENDA KNIGHT

SPIRITUAL WISDOM WALL HANGINGS

I have always loved surrounding myself with walls holding spiritual wisdom. When I was in high school, a poster reminding me that "Today is the first day of the rest of your life" was displayed alongside an image of Olympic swimmer Mark Spitz in all his seven-gold-medal splendor—each in its own way a reminder that every morning brought with it the promise of new life, new beginnings, new chapters for me to create about myself and my life. (A precocious friend at the time commented on my tendency to surround myself with words of inspiration and encouragement, noting that I was like the woman in the Dorothy Parker poem "Interior," who lives with "mottoes on the wall.")

"Creativity is a sacred universal energy, a manifestation of the divine."

—ADRIANA DIAZ

That focus hasn't changed much in the forty years that have passed since then. I look around my office today and see similar themes: an embellished collage exhorting me in Gandhi's words to "Be the change you wish to see in the world"; a painted quotation on glass from the Buddha encouraging me: "Like the moon, come out from behind the clouds. Shine!"

Though the spectrum of what words of wisdom have fed me spiritually through the years has deepened—ranging in my early twenties from a Bruce Springsteen lyric ("It ain't no sin to be glad you're alive!") to, in my mid-fifties, a Tolstoy quotation ("Grow spiritually and help others to do so. It is the meaning of life")—having visual

Looking at Patterns

"When my wife and I decided to move to the United States for her to continue her studies, I did not have a job or contacts, and our daughter was just two years old. This was an absolute leap of faith, and I was very nervous. I knew that if I did not do something constructive with my time, I was going to be all stressed out.

"We asked a friend who is an artist to draw a needlepoint pattern for me to do, something big. Of course, the first thing I did—as a good engineer—was to calculate how many stitches it would take me to finish it: around half a million. This project really made me feel relaxed while doing it; it helped me a lot to think about my situation, what was going on, my fears, my dreams.

"After working on it for a couple of months, I could see clearly the stress, the fears and my impatience on it: stitches so tight, trying to define the shape of the pattern here and there; trying to see the final result even when I was doing the first steps; some stitches more relaxed. I still can feel in my body the feelings I had when doing the needlepoint when I look at the back of the final work: My stomach contracts when I see the initial tightly sewn and dispersed patches, and my chest opens when I see the final stitches that are long, even, and relaxed. Those were the moments when I knew it was not 'just a craft'—there is something more, something deeper, involved in the process.

"At the beginning it was just a form of activity to do something good with my time, and maybe something pretty to give to my family or friends. It was something really private at the beginning—after all, the common idea seems to be that men don't do crafts unless it involves using heavy tools or welding something.

"One interesting part of my crafting in the last three or four years has been choosing a type of craft that gives more room to uncertainty. My first models made on paper were drawn on paper with grid lines; being exact in the measures was really important. Now, my needlework done with beading is more loose: sometimes the beads are not exactly uniform in size or length, so there is more room to experiment and to not have a clear idea of the final result. Sometimes, the empty spaces are the parts that fill the work.

"I think beading really opened my mind and spirit to be in a place where things cannot be totally planned ahead and where I can try and undo my work or enjoy the small 'imperfections' or uncertainty of the whole project. I really feel that through the process of adding, little by little, the small beads that become part of the whole work, my expectations start to fade and the track of time also gets lost.

"And that's the guidance I would give someone who wants to start crafting as a spiritual practice: Drop the expectations; give it time to complete the whole process; make 'errors' or the unexpected *part* of the process. Tibetan sand mandalas were an eye-opener for me: so much patience, so much beauty created, and then they are taken back to a heap of sand, to remind us of impermanence. That has been something powerful for me.

"If you're a man, know that you're not alone. When new people come to my home and see my crafts around the place, they always congratulate my wife and she has to tell them that it was me who made them. At least I get the credit at the end! I wanted to post pictures of my crafts in Flickr, for my family to see them, but I was a little concerned about making them public. Then I found a group in Flickr called 'Manbroidery,' for crafts made by men; the picture on the main page of the group shows a man doing embroidery while smoking. That made me laugh and join the group immediately—this group has been an inspiration to break the stereotype of 'women only' when crafting."

—VLADIMIR SANCHEZ

representations of inspirational words around me has remained a constant practice. It is a way to keep my intentions before me and to remember what's most important to me; it encourages me, on a daily basis, to be mindful of the potential that each day holds for transformation; and it reminds me, in the words of poet Emily Dickinson, to "dwell in possibility."

Inner Inquiries for Journaling and Reflection

✴ What spiritual sayings—or "mottoes"—have heart and meaning for me right now? In what ways am I living up to those words (or not living up to them)?

✴ What words would I like to share as an inspirational saying? What message is it that I most want to impart to the world?

DIY: Crafting a Spiritual Wisdom Wall Hanging

If you, too, are nourished by actually seeing the letters and words that comprise a favorite piece of spiritual wisdom, then there are a number of ways that you can create a wall hanging. Whether paper or fabric, collaged or assemblaged, beaded or built, your spiritual wisdom phrase will inform—and be informed by—the materials you choose.

Sacred Bath Salts

Back in the early '70s, when I was a teenager, the promise of a bath boasting Calgon products was an invitation to an altered state; "Calgon, take me away!" seemed almost an incantation. That advertising slogan touched something deep; it has been so successful that it remains in use today and the manufacturer even has a corresponding website (www.takemeaway.com)! In company promotional materials, Calgon states its dedication to "creating uniquely exhilarating bath and body experiences that stimulate the senses, restore the spirit, and take you on a special, fragrant journey to the place you want to be...[the product] has always been about taking you away on your journey."

Stimulating the senses, restoring the spirit, and taking you on a special, fragrant journey—clearly, there is a deep association with bathing and transcendence, which is not surprising, given bathing's ancient roots as a spiritual practice. In most cultures and many religions, throughout time, bathing has been seen as a means of purification and cleansing. Baptism as practiced by Christians is mirrored by the ancient water ritual of Hindus, who go to the Ganges River to immerse themselves; the spiritual bathing ritual for purification known as Mikvah that is practiced by Jews is mirrored by the Buddhist practice of spiritual bathing, also for purification, in order to connect with a Higher Power.

Knowing that you are taking part in a ritual that

"To live and love, to give expression to it...one must also be a true believer. There must be something to worship. Where in this broad land is the holy of holies hidden?"

—HENRY MILLER

has ancient roots among peoples around the world, crafting sacred bath salts as spiritual practice can help you feel connected not only to God but also to all the brothers and sisters of our world. You can use your ritual bath to cleanse yourself of negative energy or to attract something to you (by bathing, it is said, during a waxing moon).

You can also explore praying during a bath—what better way to be in the presence of God than alone, without distraction; your nakedness then becomes a metaphor for showing up without artifice in the presence of the Holy. After learning a particular body prayer using my arms in a workshop, I found myself repeating the movements in my bath—the warmth of the water, the sounds of the little lapping waves, the smell of the fragrant bath salts all added up to deep, abiding comfort.

If this calls to you as a craft to explore as a spiritual practice, refer to the chart on the next page to see what fragrances will best support your spiritual intention. Crafting the salts and creating a ritual to use them will shift your bathtime from a daily duty to a daily devotion. May the Divine "take you away" to the place you pray to be!

Essential Oil Properties

The following essential oils have been used to promote happiness and peace; these might also be helpful for making your own anointing oils. Please remember to do your homework before using essential oils; do not apply undiluted essential oils onto the skin. Use extreme caution when using oils with children, and if you are pregnant or have any medical problem; in these cases, a qualified aromatherapy practitioner should be consulted for proper guidance.

Bergamot: Mood-lifter; can soothe anger or frustration
Frankincense: Elevates the mind; relieves tension and fear
Geranium: Balancing; helps with connecting to intuition
Grapefruit: Uplifts; helps with resentment and envy
Lemon: Mood-lifter; helps with trust and feelings of security
Neroli: Calms; helps with anxiety, depression, and stress
Rose: Creates a sense of well-being, balance, and harmony
Sandalwood: Uplifts; helps with relaxation
Ylang Ylang: Calming; helps to soothe anger and over-excitement

Looking at Patterns

"I knit and/or needlepoint (not at the same time of course) as a spiritual practice. It's very soothing and spiritual. It quiets me, calms me down. It's a time for me to gather my thoughts, and 'be still.' There are many times I've prayed or conversed with God while knitting. When in between larger projects, I always knit a quick washcloth. I love having those on hand for incidental 'love gifts' when needed. That and a great bar of delicious soap make a great pick-me-up. I never ever feel guilty about checking out and pulling out my project. In a 'far too busy world,' it gives me a chance to unplug, reenergize, and gain the right focus."

–SHERRYE THREADGILL MACHA

Inner Inquiries for Journaling and Reflection

✳   What do I need to cleanse myself of right now? What would I like to "scrub off" and out of my life?

✳   Am I taking enough time to soak in, soak up, to simply soak…in a bath, in a lazy Saturday, in my life?

"If, indeed, truth is beauty and beauty truth, then the monk and the artist are one. Monasticism, in fact, cultivates the artistic spirit. Basic to monasticism are the very qualities art demands of the artist: silence, contemplation, discernment of spirits, community, and humility. Basic to art are the very qualities demanded of the monastic: single-mindedness, beauty, immersion, praise, and creativity. The merger of one with the other makes for great art; the meaning of one for the other makes for great soul."

–JOAN CHITTESTER

DIY: Crafting a Sacred Bath Salt

To make three cups of bath salts, combine two cups of Epsom salts with one cup of salt—coarse, rock, or sea salt—in a large glass or metal mixing bowl. If desired, add food coloring (two to three drops) and/or essential oil (five to six drops) for color and fragrance (add the desired amount of food coloring before the fragrance oil, and mix well). One-quarter to one teaspoon of glycerin can also be added for its moisturizing qualities; if you choose to use glycerin, mix it into the salt mixture before adding color and fragrance.

Use one-third to one-half a cup for each bath; store the unused salts in a lidded glass container.

TABLETOP MEDITATION FOUNTAINS

What is it about the sound of running water that produces such a state of serenity? For almost everybody, it does—and there have been some experiments by researchers that seem to back up what we've always instinctively known: the sound of water is healing, and can measurably reduce our stress levels.

In the last fifteen years, sales of tabletop meditation fountains have risen steadily—in 1998, only a hundred thousand were sold; as we moved into the twenty-first century, that number had increased to more than three million annually. Why have these indoor fountains become so popular? The answer to that question can be found by simply tuning in to the ambient noise around us at any given time—our busy modern lives are attended by sounds of all kinds, many of them unpleasant: car horns, slamming doors, people talking on cell phones. The sound of trickling water can help us to focus on that, instead; and with that shift in focus, our minds can become calmed.

Thus, a tabletop meditation fountain can become a craft that keeps on giving—if you decide to explore making your own fountain, you will find spiritual rewards involving almost all of our human senses. By choosing crystals, special stones, or spiritual figurines to place in your fountain, you are creating a living altar that will be a feast for your eyes. By listening to the sounds of your fountain, you will give your mind the opportunity to rest and your heart the chance to be reminded of nature's wonderful watery delights: waterfalls, rain, rivers. Most importantly, you will give your spirit the opportunity to dwell with God—as that wonderful verse in the Book of Isaiah put it, "to be like a flowing spring whose waters never run dry."

Inner Inquiries for Journaling and Reflection

* What does the flow of water have to tell me about my life right now?

* What other memories of the sound of running water soothe my soul?

* How can I create more "flow" in my attitudes, my art, my schedule?

DIY: Crafting a Tabletop Meditation Fountain

To make your own tabletop meditation fountain, start with a ceramic container or bowl that supports your meditation intention—perhaps it will be in the shape of a flower, or be a color that soothes you. It should be between eight to twelve inches in diameter and at least four inches deep. (Buy a container that does not have a hole in it, and be sure the depth is sufficient to cover the pump. If possible, buy a pump that has a suction cup to keep it in place.) You'll need a small water pump (aquarium pumps work well for this purpose) that pumps less than a hundred gallons per hour; also buy plastic tubing with a five-eighths-inch outer dimension.

Then comes the fun part: choosing what elements you will want to place in your fountain: a special heart-shaped rock? pebbles from a faraway beach? an amethyst crystal or tiny geode? a colored shell or interesting piece of driftwood? What about adding a plant or a small figurine? (I have an ivory-colored Quan Yin, a flat amethyst stone, and a rock printed with the word "pray" in mine.) Whatever special elements you choose will add to the meaning and intention of your fountain.

Place the submersible pump in the bottom of your container, and add enough water to cover it; otherwise, the pump will burn out. Plug it in (this will need to be near the back of your fountain) to make sure it's working. Add larger rocks to fill the bottom, and use smaller ones to decorate the top, which will be seen. Fill the container with stones, leaving an inch from the top, and arranging them in such a way that the water will flow in a pleasing sound to your ears. Once the stones are in place, you can add the accents—the crystals, shells, or figurines that are meaningful to you.

After you've made your fountain, check the water level daily; if there is too much water, you can remove it with a turkey baster, and if there is too little, add more to ensure that the pump stays covered. To keep the water running clear, add a small amount of bleach and make sure to clean the components of your fountain every month to remove any algae that might have built up. (You should take the fountain apart and clean each element about every three months.)

Flashes of Inspiration

"Though playing the guitar and singing might not be classified as crafts, they have been a method of spiritual practice, especially when playing for a listening audience. My best performances are when I get into a 'zone' and something connects me to the audience that feels greater than the sum of the parts. I still retain my individuality and ability to control my actions, but things also feel 'aligned' somehow. Playing and singing then become much more effortless. I refrain from using the word *spiritual* as that is way overused, but it's the closest way I ever get to it. I can sometimes experience it playing alone, but it is strongest with others listening. My favorite description of this is found in the Huna works by Max Freedom Long."

–DAVE JOHNSON

"The act of creating is a healing gesture, as sacred as prayer, as essential to the spirit as food to the body."

–JAN PHILLIPS

CRAFTING FOR CLARITY

Chapter 2:

CRAFTING FOR CLARITY

"Sometimes illuminations visit us at the center of meditation and prayer as
God shines light on our path and in our hearts, but they can come at any
time, in any place, and through any means—even a yellow crayon."
–KARLA M. KINCANNON

CLARITY—FROM LATIN AND FRENCH ROOTS MEANING
clearness, to make clear. Twenty-first-century life does not give us many opportunities
for cultivating clarity; indeed, conversely, many things seem muddied, too complex. But
in the practice of addressing our art materials for the sake of becoming more clear—
whether that means a deeper understanding of a question or a calling, or simply a time to
un-wad the crinkles of a too-busy mind—we can find illumination.

Yet, as Anaïs Nin reminds us, "There are very few human beings who receive the
truth, complete and staggering, by instant illumination. Most of them acquire it fragment by fragment on a small scale, by successive developments, cellularly, like a laborious

mosaic"—and what better way than through the steps of a craft to build this inner mosaic of understanding?

> "Art is an intuitive act of the spirit in its evolution toward divine nature."
> —M. C. RICHARDS

In this chapter we will look at five practices that lend themselves more than others to clearing the waters, to shedding light on what it is that our lives may be calling to bear fruit: collage treasure maps, visual journals, personal prayer flags, blessing baskets, and creating a spiritual toolbox. When exploring the possibilities of these crafts for creating clarity, remember that it is in the process, the doing, that answers can be found; as the German proverb suggests, "Begin to weave, and God will give you the thread."

COLLAGE TREASURE MAPS

Picture this: a long rectangle of poster board, slightly bigger than a panorama photograph, embellished with silver and fuchsia glitter-glue spirals. On it are images of the Golden Gate Bridge, a couple walking on the beach, an open hand, a small advertisement for the movie *Fearless*,

> "As we embark on a new creative venture, it helps to remember that we are working with a God who loves us more than anything in the world."
>
> —ELLEN MORRIS PREWITT

and words torn from magazine ads: "break the rules," "go with your heart," "the world is wide," "anything can happen." This is the collage treasure map that I made and placed on my dresser top, and looked at every day, *feeling* myself in those scenarios of the City by the Bay.

It was 1994, and I was living in Indianapolis, feeling increasingly restless and unhappy. I truly had left my heart in San Francisco, a city I'd known was my *real* home from my first visit there at the age of twenty-one. I had continued my visits there into my thirties but still hadn't made the actual leap into living there.

The restlessness I was feeling turned into an insistence that I *must* move to San Francisco—an insistence so urgent that it almost felt like a matter of life and death. I turned to the practice of treasure-mapping—which I'd learned about in a Unity church, at a workshop in which we discovered the power of visual images in keeping people's deepest goals and intentions before them—to see what would turn up in visual form, to explore this call to move that was coming from my very soul.

A short four months later, I had received a wonderful and unlikely job offer at a nonprofit organization in Sausalito, California, which, for a San Francisco resident, required a daily commute across the Golden Gate Bridge, the biggest and central image in my collage. In my now-eighteen years of living in San Francisco, which still feels like my true home, I met my husband (remember that image of a couple on the beach?) and have had many more dreams come true: becoming a mother, a minister, and the author of books including this one. I've certainly become more fearless…and have learned through the big and little miracles of my life that, indeed, anything can happen. Collage treasure maps have played a part in all these dreams-come-true.

As *Simple Abundance* author Sarah Ban Breathnach wrote about her experience with creating collage treasure maps, "This is a meditative insight tool as well as a playmate, which means you want to bring your full concentration to each collage. Remember that these are the illustrations of your soul's autobiography. This is the first rough draft of your magnum opus…discovering who we are and why we are here at this point in eternity."

Inner Inquiries for Journaling and Reflection

✳ What are my deepest hopes for my life? What do I want to create in and for my life?

✳ Do I honor all the pieces and parts—whole and torn, vibrant and "ugly"—of my life?

* Do I honor all the pieces and parts—whole and torn, vibrant and "ugly"—of myself?

* How can I begin to see the perfection in the imperfection? What would help me right now to see my life as a collage, full of disparate bits that connect together to make a unified whole?

* What do I need to do to create order and beauty from seeming randomness? What do I need to put into my life—or leave out?

DIY: Crafting a Collage Treasure Map

To make your own treasure map, you'll need a field. Through the years I have made treasure maps of every size and shape, on mason board, foam core, and poster board, big (a poster board heart) and small (on a three-by-five index card). Allow yourself time to pray or meditate on what intention you want your treasure map to hold. In silence, go through a stack of magazines that you don't mind cutting up and pull from the pages images and phrases that speak to you. When you feel complete, begin to tear or cut out those images and words (I've heard it said that tearing around an image rather than cutting around it can access deeper places in the unconscious) and place them on your field, later gluing them into the positions that feel right to you. Embellish with glitter glue or other elements if you like. Place your collage treasure map on a personal altar or in another setting where you can see it every day.

Guides for the Path

The following books may be helpful to you in exploring collage treasure maps as a spiritual practice:

The Vision Board: The Secret to an Extraordinary Life by Joyce Schwarz (Collins Design, 2008)

Visioning: Ten Steps to Designing the Life of Your Dreams by Lucia Capacchione (Tarcher/Putnam, 2000)

The Illustrated Discovery Journal: Creating a Visual Autobiography of Your Authentic Self by Sarah Ban Breathnach (Warner Books, 1999)

Looking at Patterns

"When I was in my mid-thirties, I really got interested in collage and began to use words, phrases, and images as a way of manifesting what I wanted in my life. Often it was the means by which I came to *know* what I wanted in my life—accessing my inner knowing through the right brain. Eventually I came to see the collage process as a form of prayer.

"More than a decade later, my husband and I attended a communications training in southern California. In one of the classes, our teacher led a series of meditations, culminating in an image of a rider approaching from the distance, carrying an important message from The King, for my eyes alone. The message was said to connect to some facet of my life purpose. In this case, the message was, 'Manifest Healing Through Creative Self-expression.' Then she asked us to write down a number of steps we could take to fulfill this mission and then to choose one that we could do right away when we got home. I wrote down that I could teach collage classes to groups of emotionally challenged people.

"On the second day after we returned home, my friend Monica called. She knew someone who was looking for a teacher for crafts classes in a residence for people with HIV. I said 'yes!' without hesitation. There was no question that the Universe was answering my invitation. I started teaching classes right away.

"One student was intensely shy and nervous. He did not talk or seem to connect with the others during the classes at all. He always arrived after the class started and left before our show-and-tell. He hid his work from the view of the others and never asked for help from anyone. He had been in the class for more than a year and it was always like that with him. He was so consistent that no one even questioned his ways.

"This one day he prepared his page almost entirely upside down! His paper was face down on the table, except when he was pasting something on it and then he'd flip it right back down. Then, at the end of the class, he didn't leave before the show-and-tell. Rather he continued to work on his art without looking up or speaking. When everyone left the room, he remained in his seat while I cleaned up. I looked at him and he held my gaze, although I could see it was an effort for him to do it. He then did the most surprising thing: He held up his art to show me what he had done. His paper had many faces collaged all over it. He gestured to the page and (he only spoke Spanish) said, '*Muchas sonrisas*' ('Many smiles'). And I noticed that almost all the faces on the page were smiling. Then he gestured around the room and said, '*Todos sonriendo*' ('Everyone is smiling'). Then he pointed to one face on his collage at the lower central part of the page. This one face was not smiling. And he said, '*Excepto yo. Estoy tieso*' ('Except me. I'm stiff'). I responded with an empathic, slightly sad look and a nod. I had no words and none seemed necessary or helpful. He left the room looking intently at his page.

"At the next class meeting, he came in before the class started—with the rest of the group—and took his seat. During the class, he sat a little more back from his work, not shielding it from view quite so much. I was very touched when he asked someone to pass a glue stick, rather than getting up and walking around to get it for himself, as he usually would have done. And so it went for the next several classes before the group disbanded.

"It has happened over and over again that I am collaging a certain situation or mood, and I see myself—my role—through my collage. I can see the part I'm playing and how I am creating or participating in the dynamic around me. It's very instrumental to personal growth and that is what my student experienced that day, in that class. He was transformed. Even if it only meant that he would ask someone to pass a glue stick instead of getting up and walking around to get it himself; he had an inner experience that was a great gift, not only to himself, but to the rest of the group as well. *A Course in Miracles* says, 'When I am healed, I am not healed alone.' And I believe that this is an example of that principle.

"Currently I'm teaching an Art Journaling class. We use collage techniques in blank art books. We use images (mostly from magazines) to represent the moods, activities, seasons, and events of our lives. The pages often have a deep personal meaning for the artist, and often speak directly to the hearts of others as well. The images evoke different emotional responses in different people, and their arrangements, with words and colors, will suggest different meanings to different people.

"What is terribly important for me in my practice is that I make time every day to spend with my journal. At this point, I have been actively doing collage as a spiritual practice for more than twenty years and I can't imagine ever *not* doing it—almost every day! Through my collage and art journaling I find I can know myself better and I can indeed 'Manifest Healing Through Creative Self-expression'!"

—ZIEK PATERNITI

VISUAL JOURNALS

I first began making visual journals when I was in college, not knowing there was even a term for them—to me, they were just containers for saving all the wonderful pieces of life that were flying my way: a postcard of a cobalt-blue Matisse cutout, seen on a weekend trip to Manhattan; a wonderful quotation from Rilke's *Lessons to a Young Poet,* about "living the questions now"; a ticket stub from a Bruce Springsteen concert, which had provided four hours of transcendent joy. They were a celebration, a grab bag for the eyes, a profusion of personal and cultural diamonds, collected by me as my life and heart expanded with the joy of discovering a big wide world out there.

> "Every artist dips his brush in his own soul, and paints his own nature into his pictures."
>
> —HENRY WARD BEECHER

While journaling by its very nature could be considered a spiritual practice—since we are, after all, "baring our souls" in our journals—one can use specific techniques for consciously making it even more of a spiritual practice. Marianne Hieb, a Sister of Mercy who is the director of the Wellness Spirituality Program at Lourdes Wellness Center in Collingswood, New Jersey, as well as an art teacher and the author of *Inner Journeying Through Art-Journaling: Learning to See and Record Your Life as a Work of Art,* has even created a trademarked process—Art-Journaling®—through which one can uncover greater depths. Marianne describes how she was led to visual journals as a spiritual practice: "When planning a weekend retreat with a wellness spirituality theme, the staff encouraged me to include a creativity session in the format. As a result, I brought drawing paper

43

and oil pastels, writing supplies and an outline of the meditation to the weekend experi-ence. Using 'the gift of the present moment' as a theme, the retreatants considered the aspects of their ordinary days, used the pastels to create lines and shapes to express that experience, gazed at their visual expression, and then moved into a time of reflective writing. The meditation was followed by silence and optional sharing. The art-journaling prayer process as I would present and facilitate it was born."

Marianne continues: "In my definition, Art-Journaling shares in the disciplines of spiritual direction, design theory, fine art, art therapy, creativity, and the contemplative tradition. My particular approach to journaling is holistic, and includes the combination of nonverbal and verbal aspects. In my retreats and workshops, I urge participants to trust their inner wisdom, and their belief in the God who desires to reveal.

"In Art-Journaling prayer, we begin with a theme or question, respond prayerfully to that question with art materials, take some time to 'gaze contemplatively, non-judgmen-tally, receptively,' and only then does the retreatant go into the verbal journaling process. Over the years, through the graced sharing of the participants, I have learned how the combination of nonverbal and verbal approaches can yield profound and surprisingly swift insights."

Whether you work with Marianne's Art-Journaling® technique, another's (see "Guides for the Path" on the following pages), or create your own system of visual journ-aling as I did that literally includes pieces of ephemera from your day-to-day experiences, it can reveal important insights about your life—and spiritual—journey.

Inner Inquiries for Journaling and Reflection

    ❋   How do I want to use my visual journal: as an ongoing record in which to explore the spiritual dimensions of my life? as a reflection tool using specific questions for inquiry? as a place to simply "be," in which to write, draw, and color as I am moved to?

    ❋   Like the protagonist in Doris Lessing's *The Golden Notebook,* you may choose to have different journals for the various parts of your life. Ask yourself: What are the main categories that my life is currently organized into (i.e., "parent," "employee," "artist," "spiritual being," etc.)?

    ❋   Is there one category of my life that I would like to be focusing more on? Would a separate visual journal for that category be helpful to me now?

Guides for the Path

With the popularity of visual journaling, there are many published books (many by North Light Books) that will guide you through technique and offer inspiration. Among them are:

Creative Awakenings: Envisioning the Life of Your Dreams Through Art by Sheri Gaynor (North Light Books, 2009)

Journal Spilling: Mixed-Media Techniques for Free Expression by Diana Trout (North Light Books, 2009)

True Vision: Authentic Art Journaling by L. K. Ludwig (Quarry Books, 2008)

The Journal Junkies Workshop: Visual Ammunition for the Art Addict by Eric Scott and David Modler (North Light Books, 2010)

The following books focus more on visual journaling as a spiritual practice:

Inner Journeying Through Art-Journaling: Learning to See and Record Your Life as a Work of Art by Marianne Hieb (Jessica Kingsley Publishers, 2005)

The Artful Journal: A Spiritual Quest by Maureen Carey, Raymond Fox, and Jacqueline Penney (Watson-Guptill Publications, 2002)

Art Journals and Creative Healing: Restoring the Spirit Through Self-Expression by Sharon Soneff (Quarry Books, 2008)

Crafting a Spiritual Practice

"The guidance that I would give others who want to approach their craft as a spiritual practice is simply to *notice*. Depending on what the craft is, don't worry too much about the outcome, at least in terms of a spiritual practice in relation to a product; cultivate a contemplative mind and listen to the stirrings underneath the experience. Seek out skilled [artistic] guidance when you are having difficulty with the craft, and seek out spiritual and/or emotional guidance when you are being challenged or invited by the movements underneath, within, and/or beyond the craft experience.

"I think it is always a good idea to explore new media and approaches. No one holds the exclusive key to creativity—creativity is, of its nature, unique. Be wary if someone says 'This is the way to be creative'! I have learned over the years to move away from situations, systems, and individuals who declare that 'this one way' is the way—be yourself!

"Learn the rules, and then let go of them. It is important to learn everything you can about your craft, and then to come at it with a beginner's mind. You never want to lose the ability to be surprised, to surprise yourself, to learn and do something new. At the same time, there is a spirituality in discipline, repetition, a peaceful settling in. Notice."

—MARIANNE HIEB

Personal Prayer Flags

I look at the personal prayer flag that I made more than a decade ago. Fashioned out of a placemat woven in threads of persimmon, eggplant, and ochre, its elements still enchant me: a large, heavily textured silk sunflower head, a green-satin leafy stem below, embellished with tiny pearls; a gray-blue feather; a fabric square containing a color line drawing of a woman's head; a cloth bag in Provençal print spilling out tiny orange-plastic hearts; two organic, Matisse-like shapes made of fabric with shiny gold dots. Though I no longer remember the exact context in which I placed these elements, they still delight me—they still speak to me of my soul's desire to create, to celebrate beauty, to love.

Prayer flags have been used for thousands of years in Tibet; highly decorated and including written prayers or mantras, these colorful cloths are believed to waft their prayers in the wind as they wave, bestowing blessings onto everyone along that path. They are usually found in groups of five—yellow, green, red, white, and blue, connected together by a long cord and displayed either horizontally or vertically.

Why make a personal prayer flag? Let me answer that with a story: I remember once during my travels abroad, in a European city that I inexplicably felt so estranged and "other" in, rounding a corner and seeing, far down the cobblestoned

"For me, spirituality is not about separating myself from my life. It is about getting more deeply in touch with the sacred in my daily living. Human life is sacred; therefore, what we do and how we fill our lives is sacred. So when you are doing your ordinary things, tap into the sacred. Listen to your soul. Use that to make your art."

—JULIE-ANN SILBERMAN

street, a building displaying an American flag. I remember at that moment feeling a surprising sense of patriotism—that's *my* flag, I thought to myself; I'm an *American*. My heart lifted; it was a symbol of my identity; it was *home*.

Making a personal prayer flag can have the same effect—a deeper, spiritual effect—on us; for when choosing the elements for our personal prayer flag, we are identifying what makes us unique, what we honor in ourselves, what we have to give to the world... and what we spiritually identify with. We are making a symbol of our soul's home.

Inner Inquiries for Journaling and Reflection

✳   Flags have traditionally served as "the pride of a nation," a source of identification. Ask yourself: When I think about making a personal prayer flag, what colors would best express me? What symbols?

✳   What above all is my prayer for my life—what do I want my flag to stand for?

✳   What embellishments will give me a sense of *home*—my spiritual home?

49

DIY: Crafting a Personal Prayer Flag

Being somewhat textile-ly challenged myself, I prefer making prayer flags out of precut forms (cloth placemats work very well) and strong crafter's glue that will hold heavier elements such as beads or small stones. Depending on how you plan to work with your prayer flag, you will want to experiment with the size and materials that work best for that intention. You can make single flags, as I did, or, if you want to create a series of prayer flags, like the ones found in Tibet, you can create a method for stringing them by folding over the material at each flag's top and stitching it to create a half-inch tunnel through which you can thread string or cord through all of your flags, creating a unified row.

Guides for the Path

When making your prayer flag or flags, it can be helpful to know what associations certain shapes and colors have (for instance, the colors in Tibetan prayer flags represent the elements—earth, yellow; water, green; fire, red; clouds, white; and sky, blue). For a list of other associations with particular colors, see the box in the "Prayer Shawls" section.

There's also a wonderful book by Angeles Arrien on what shapes mean cross-cultur-ally; titled *Signs of Life* (Tarcher, 1998), it will guide you through the meanings of the square, circle, triangle, equidistant cross and spiral and what your attraction to any of those shapes might mean about where you are in life.

Looking at Patterns

"I made my first mezuzah cases (small cases containing a scroll with a verse from Deuteronomy that are affixed to their doorposts by some Jewish families as a sign and reminder of their faith) in 1993, one year after I began the process of learning metalsmithing. I was twenty years old, questioning my faith, a sociology major, and a sophomore in college wanting to understand how something like the Holocaust could have happened. I wanted to prevent future atrocities like this from occurring. I wanted to preserve a tradition. I wanted to know, how could there be a G-d, given the fact of the Holocaust? My first mezuzahs struck a chord within me to such a degree that I felt a need to make more.

"My need to preserve tradition was as strong as a baby's drive to crawl and then to walk. I proclaimed no faith in G-d but I knew that, as a grandchild of Holocaust survivors, every day I lived was a victory over Nazi brutality. My talent in metal was innate, as I come from a long line of precision tool and die makers and blacksmiths. Using my grandpa's hand tools, and investing any money I had, I designed my line of limited-production mezuzah cases and started my business in 1998, selling them to individuals and stores around the country.

"About eight years after making my first cases, I began to study the text on the mezuzah scroll. That's when I went through a spiritual transformation. I felt that the Sh'ma and V'hafta prayers were profound and universal, and that the mezuzah was a gift from G-d, reminding us of how to create sacred space, and ultimately a peaceful world. I designed a tag that would accompany each mezuzah, sharing the teaching, so that any human being who wanted to understand and use the mezuzah as part of their personal spiritual practice could. To be honest, nothing makes me feel more important than making Judaica (except for being a wife and a mother to my three-year-old son). It is an honor, and it helps me give positive meaning to my family's experience as survivors of the Holocaust.

"Personally, I believe that the teachings within Judaism are universal. The Source of Life (G-d) is the same for everyone, regardless of faith affiliation. I use my Judaica to share with people of all faiths how we Jews see G-d—as being everywhere and a part of everything; that there is a vast oneness here on earth; and that we are all interconnected. I want to create a peaceful world through the making of Judaica. Once I began this spiritual path, why would I want to make anything else?

"I make jewelry of the Hebrew letter *shin* because the meanings are universal: shaddai, protection; Shekhinah, feminine presence of G-d; sh'ma, not just "hear" but *understand in your heart*, and of course shalom, peace."

—AIMEE GOLANT

BLESSING BASKETS

Many years ago, I overheard one of my teachers and mentors—the cross-cultural anthropologist Angeles Arrien, whose book *Signs of Life* I mentioned in the previous section—counseling a friend of mine to put one of those life lessons we all receive into her "learning basket." This idea of a metaphorical basket stayed with me, and I was delighted when my friend later told me that she was going to make an actual "learning basket" to use in ritual and as a reminder to be gentle with herself as she grows and evolves.

Years later, I found myself returning to the idea of a basket as I struggled with the many time-consuming, and sometimes conflicting, roles that I played (and still play) in my life: mother of a young child, wife, care-giving daughter, care-giving professional, writer/creator, and more. I found that it helped me to think of my different roles as separate "baskets," to do what I can when I can, and then put the basket away, knowing that it will be picked up at another time, on another day.

> "What if everybody in the first grade was taught that we are Divine Beings, each of us holding a unique gift to give that can bring forward the ecstasy when we share the gift with others? What is more important than this? This sharing of ourselves, the loving others through our unique talents, *this* is our daily bread."
>
> —KATHERINE Q. REVOIR

Yet another association for a basket came later from Angeles, in a conversation about holding our tangible and intangible gifts in a "blessing basket." Again, that image stayed with me and I bought a tiny, handwoven basket from an artisan at a craft fair to anchor that sense of gratitude within me: Only two-and-a-half inches square, the basket is woven with strips of dried grass, woolen yarn, and ocean-blue metallic thread; on either side, strings hold an abundance of beads and charms in every conceivable color and shape—a hematite heart, a brass butterfly, an iridescent star. To me, it is a perfect representation of a blessing basket—reminding me that blessings can be tiny, and discovered in the world every day.

As Meister Eckhart once wrote, "If the only prayer you ever say in your life is 'thank you,' that will be enough." Expressing gratitude on a daily basis, being thankful for the blessings in our lives, is considered to be one of the most powerful spiritual practices we can undertake. If you make a blessing basket, reflect on ways you could integrate it into your everyday schedule—perhaps you could fill it with strips of paper listing an individual blessing of your life, and pull a strip daily to then meditate on that particular blessing. Or perhaps you could fill it each evening with a list of five things you were grateful for that day. However you decide to work with your blessing basket as a spiritual practice, the simple act of saying "thank you" will be enough.

Inner Inquiries for Journaling and Reflection

✳   What are the biggest blessings of my life?

✳   Do I express my gratitude for those blessings?

✳   How can I integrate a gratitude practice into my daily life?

DIY: Crafting a Blessing Basket

Baskets can be made in almost every material you can think of: paper (in which strips are woven together or constructed with origami folds), fabric (in which cloth is rolled to make coils, then stitched together), and the traditional way—by weaving together plant material, such as palm leaves. If you are interested in a particular technique for making your blessing basket, there are a number of useful books (and even kits) for doing so that you will find with an Internet search.

But to begin your practice immediately, another way to create a blessing basket is simply to embellish a pre-existing basket that you feel drawn to, using paint, ribbon, charms, and anything else that evokes blessings for you. Remember—as with all the crafts that we're exploring—that what's most important is not the actual crafting of the basket, but the spiritual practice behind it.

SPIRITUAL TOOLBOXES

As artists and craftspeople, we know the joy inherent in supplies—who reading this hasn't gotten excited over a brand-new unopened sketchbook, a tin of pristine water-colors, or tubes of glitter glue in every color of the rainbow? It's that "new box of sixty-four crayons" feeling that never fails to delight. And after hearing a friend talk about the tools—the tools of living a successful, resourceful life—that were in her personal "toolbox," I became intrigued by the idea of actually creating a toolbox, containing supplies—like my art supplies—that I could access within. Though for me, the toolbox I wanted to create was a spiritual toolbox.

Creating a spiritual toolbox is an ongoing practice, for as we age, grow, and evolve, that which nourishes us spiritually sometimes begins to transition too. Crafters who are drawn to this practice will enjoy making their own toolboxes, perhaps out of wood or tin; for others less mechanically talented (like me), the practice will lie in the embellishment of a pre-made toolbox.

> "The transformation comes from engaging in the work, of practicing being present to the moment and what it has to teach you about yourself, your creative process, and God."
>
> —CHRISTINE VALTERS PAINTNER

The one I chose was found in a drugstore and designed to hold makeup; it is composed of indigo plastic with silver glitter embedded within it—conjuring images of stars at night. Though the actual material isn't soul satisfying, the transparent pocket on the front of it is—perfect for a small collage treasure map or photograph that can change (and has changed) through the years. Inside are tiny compartments with a mirrored inside lid, the mirror a reminder that all the "tools" are a reflection of the inner resources I carry within.

Elements I've included in my personal spiritual toolbox include a miniature copy of *As a Man Thinketh*, the classic book by James Allen on the power of disciplining our minds (later added to this was *As a Woman Thinketh,* a small booklet by Dorothy J. Hulst that changed Allen's original patriarchal languaging), as well as small charms, tokens, and trinkets that each remind me of the spiritual strengths that I can draw upon.

The saxophonist John Coltrane once said, "My goal is to live the truly religious life and express it through my music. My music is the spiritual expression of what I am, my faith, my knowledge, and my being." Crafting a spiritual toolbox can help you to explore what you are, what your faith is, what your knowledge is, and what you associate with your very being. See if you can find those symbols, and add them to your toolbox.

Inner Inquiries for Journaling and Reflection

* What *are* the tools that I carry in my "spiritual toolbox"? What best symbolizes each tool?

* Does anything in my spiritual toolbox surprise me? What spiritual tools do I use the most? What spiritual tool(s) do I need to develop?

* Which craft is my most favorite spiritual tool?

Looking at Patterns

"Yarn shops are holy places, and I don't mean that irreverently or flippantly. Truly, I approach them with reverence. I wander their aisles in quiet wonder. For me there is a sacredness about those stacks and piles of fiber, dyed in every color you can imagine, and some you couldn't. There is magic in the textures and my hands reach out to feel every single one: the smoothness of silks, the scratch and slight oiliness of Shetland wools, the coolness of cotton, the airy cloud of angora. Alpaca, merino, bamboo, they're all miraculous in their power to inspire.

"That's the thing about working with fiber, the inspiration that comes from the medium. I imagine it's akin to the way a sculptor can see the form in wood or stone just waiting to be carved. Yarn will tell you what it wants to be. If you listen carefully you'll hear. Lately it's been whispering to me about forms that are decidedly nonfunctional. I feel myself preparing to embark on something new, something more sculptural. I don't know quite what form it will take, but it's tugging on my sleeve, trying to get my attention. But I know I'll never give up my useful creations entirely, no matter what other inspirations await me. There is something too wonderful about seeing my daughter in the jacket I made for her, or seeing my husband reach over and over again for the sweater that I worked on for months. Or watching my son snuggle up on the couch with the pillows I wove. It's like there's a magic spell stitched and woven into these things

I make for people. Like an amulet worn for protection.

"I have, like most ardent knitters, a stash. It's huge. I don't know how many balls, cones, and skeins of yarn I have. But it fills completely a six-foot-tall, two-foot-wide cabinet. Sometimes the doors pop open by themselves. Then there are the baskets on top of the cabinet, and on top of the two book-shelves as well. They're all stuffed with yarn, too. Oh, and one on the floor behind my loom, too. That has some odds and ends in it as well. It's probably about time to sort through it and find some yarn to give away, not of course because I want to have less yarn. Oh no! I want to have more. I need to make room for new stuff.

"People who don't knit, crochet, or weave don't really understand the need to stockpile yarn. I can accept that it's a little strange. I could stop buying yarn now and I probably wouldn't run out for years. People would say, 'You can't take it with you.' And I know that's true. Which means I have a lot of knitting and weaving to do between now and then. But if I can't take my stash with me, does that mean there are yarn shops in heaven? There must be. Otherwise how could you call it heaven? And you know what, I bet the yarn there is amazing. And you know what else? I bet it's all free. Now that *would* be heaven."

—TARA CONNOR

> "Take your needle, my child, and work at your pattern; it will come out a rose by and by. Life is life that; one stitch at a time taken patiently, and the pattern will come out all right, like embroidery."
>
> —OLIVER WENDELL HOLMES

"Art, much like meditation, invites me inward as far as I wish to go. It is here that the voice of the Self, the divine inner realm, can be entered, observed, and expressed in manifest form."

—MICHAEL FRANKLIN

CRAFTING FOR COMFORT

Chapter 3:

CRAFTING FOR COMFORT

"The very act of creating is an act of power...of hope. It's a reminder
that we are not powerless pawns, not cattle in a big cosmic slaughter-
house. Writing a song or drawing the vase with the wilted delphiniums is
a reminder that we can do something...that we have the power to make
something from nothing. And, as those reminders add up, as hope begins
to grow, we no longer feel overwhelmed by our troubles, by the troubles of
the world. We remember that we, as humans, as cocreators with God, have
an immense power to change things."

−PAM GROUT

WHILE CRAFTING FOR COMFORT WILL CONTAIN MANY ELEMENTS
similar to crafting for calm, there is a slight difference: crafts that induce calmness have
more of a physiological effect on our bodies, while crafts that comfort are marked by their
ability to soothe our mind and heart.

As writer Karla M. Kincannon expressed it, "Participating in the creative act helps us
to see ourselves as we are and as we might become. Like prayer, the creative act draws
us into the authentic life that awaits us and into our fulfillment in God. Creativity,

an essential tool for shaping the soul, provides a pathway to the fierce truth of our life. Those traveling the spiritual road who yearn for the healing of life's deepest hurts, the fulfillment of immeasurable longings, or the profound peace found only in life with God need all their creativity to complete the journey."

> "Serving an art fulfills our deepest needs to be heard, to be visible, to shout a holy 'yes' to the miraculous that's every day around us."
>
> —PAM GROUT

And as we find comfort within the process of our creativity, others may find comfort in the product; each of the five crafts explored in this chapter—portable shrines, prayer shawls, affirmation blankets, prayer cards, and power pouches—are potent as personal practices, but also extend that quality of comfort when given away as an offering to another.

PORTABLE SHRINES

You may be carrying elements of a portable shrine with you already, though you may not think of them as such—a sacred symbol on a keychain, a good-luck talisman in your purse or on your dashboard, even a collection of photographs of your beloveds on an iPhone are all, in a sense, potential subjects of a portable shrine.

The word *shrine* comes from a Latin root meaning "case, chest," so, technically speaking, the elements of your shrine should be encased or contained in some way. Cultures from around the world have practiced the art of portable shrines in wonderful (and wonderfully creative) ways; in Mexico and Peru, tiny little folded "wallets" include good-luck seeds and photos of saints.

Another format often used in Central and South American countries is tiny matchboxes. I bought a tiny Guatemalan fabric-covered matchbox at an import store for $1.99; on the brightly striped fabric is a small seal that reads "Emergency Kit." Inside this sweet little shrine is a "worry doll," a red seed, and a clay angel pendant. The label glued to the bottom of the box explains that, "There are moments in which you need a peaceful vibe, a touch of good luck, and someone to tell your worries to. Use this emergency kit to balance those tough moments! An angel for peaceful thoughts, a Lucky Bean, and a Worry Doll."

So what calls to you to be included in your emergency kit, your portable shrine? What

> "Our vocation is not simply to be, but to work together with God in the creation of our own life, our own identity, our own destiny."
> —THOMAS MERTON

will bring you back to center when you look at or touch it—what will bring you back to the Divine? And in an interesting twist on this practice, Shaun McNiff, in his book *Trust the Process: An Artist's Guide to Letting Go*, suggests making a shrine to something or someone you don't love—as a way to work through complicated feelings: "reframing discontents into something new and creative." As he writes, "When we use our disturbances as materials of expression we see that everything in life is fuel for the creative process. Creativity puts toxins to good use."

Whether a shrine to that which you love or that which you wish to heal, making a portable shrine of tiny reminders can be powerful both in the creating, and in the carrying, of it. You may find, too, that the elements of your portable shrine change with time, and you may find joy in making them for one of those people whose photograph is on your iPhone.

Inner Inquiries for Journaling and Reflection

✳ What do I need in my spiritual "emergency kit"? What best symbolizes that which gives me the most comfort?

✳ What brings me comfort on a daily basis? What do I always want
   to have at hand?

✳ Is there anything in my life that I need to "contain"?

DIY: *Crafting a Portable Shrine*

Given the array of packaging that we are privy to in our Western world, there are a multitude of cast-off items that can be used to make a portable shrine: breath-mint tins with a hinged lid and empty matchboxes are tops on the list. (While my creative clutter causes me a pinch of shame, I have a healthy self-regard as a recycler, because the two go together, at least in the World of Craft. So I have an ever-growing pile of little boxes with hinged lids—square Green Tea Mint boxes, and round Espresso Pillow boxes, from Trader Joe's; both regular- and mini-sized Altoids boxes; velvet and faux-leather boxes once holding jewelry—all are perfect for creating portable shrines or altars.)

With a coat of white paint or gesso, your chosen surface becomes a blank canvas for whatever outside embellishment you might want to add: collaged images, a row of ribbon or sequins, alphabet beads.

And what to put inside? That's what makes this spiritual craft even more spiritual—the decisions one makes about what to include, what to carry with oneself as one journeys through life. As they say in Spanish-speaking countries, *Viva la Vida!*

Guides for the Path

The following books will be helpful in exploring portable or tabletop shrines as a spiritual practice:

Making Shadow Boxes and Shrines by Kathy Cano-Murillo (Rockport Publishers, 2002)

Crafting Personal Shrines: Using Photos, Mementos & Treasures to Create Artful Displays by Carol Owen (Lark Books, 2004)

PRAYER SHAWLS

Practicing the path of The Way of the Crafter also involves discovering what art forms *aren't* vehicles for sustained spiritual concentration. There are a number of crafts that I will never master (or even be mediocre at)—though even my thwarted attempts to learn them brought their own forms of spiritual learning. I learned this most pointedly after enrolling in a knitting class for the sole purpose of making a prayer shawl; having read about those with a prayer-shawl ministry—those who with clacking needles and nimble fingers weave magnificent, warm, and soul-pleasing pieces out of brilliantly hued yarns—I wanted with all of my heart to join their ranks. It took about ten minutes to find out that I would never be one of them, and a week later—after having even invested in a copy of *Knitting for Dummies* (a double defeat because of its humiliating title)—I sadly concluded that this is one foray into crafting that will always be doomed to failure.

That's what made my discovery of Judith Pruess-Mellow's prayer shawls such a solace, and a delight. When Judith had business that would bring her regularly to San Francisco, we would meet in a Border's café on a monthly basis to have coffee and chat; and we did this through the arc of time that began with my preparations of a detailed adoption dossier through my first months as a delighted (but tired) new mother.

One visit, Judith brought me a cherished present for my baby daughter: a prayer shawl—made of pastel-striped cotton in shades of robin's egg blue, magenta, butter yellow, and pink. It was decorated on each side with two muslin pockets that had been lovingly illustrated in crayon and colored pencil; each pocket's childlike illustration also included a special message: "Trust in God!" and "Someone will always love you!"

If you, like me, are a frustrated or failed knitter, take heart: Prayer shawls can be made from fabric, and Judith has generously shared the instructions for how to do so (see the next page). Judith has also found through time that one element of the prayer shawl—the pockets—also make wonderful stand-alone projects. Touchingly, she witnessed firsthand how dear these pockets could become to someone, when her husband was hospitalized after a stroke. His prayer pocket—embroidered with the words "Rest...All is well"—held his eyeglasses, notes of comfort, and other meaningful items, and never left his side.

> "The word 'worship' comes from an old word meaning, 'to shape things of worth.' One aspect of worship is transformation, transforming the ordinary into the Sacred, the remnant into the Holy. For me, quilting as spiritual discipline is giving shape and color and texture to my inner life. It is about making beauty from what is at hand."
>
> —LAURIE BUSHBAUM

71

What do you—or someone close to you—need to hold on to right now? A prayer shawl (or prayer pocket) may help...to literally feel the touch of Love.

Inner Inquiries for Journaling and Reflection

* What colors call to me right now? What colors do I associate with the Divine? What colors would support my prayer life?

* What quotation or wisdom verse helps me to love more? Pray more? Trust more?

DIY: Crafting a Fabric Prayer Shawl

1. You will need a piece of loosely flowing fabric, such as a rayon blend, cut to about two feet by four feet. Approximations are fine. Consider picking a fabric in healing colors—light greens, blues, pinks, lavenders, yellows—for your shawl.
2. Hem the edges of the fabric.
3. Your shawl will have two pockets, one at either end, which consist of eight-and-a-half-by-eleven-inch pieces of muslin. After they have been decorated (see below), the pockets should be hemmed and sewn on three sides to the large (shawl) piece of fabric. The opening for the pocket is toward the center of the shawl, so that when one is wearing the prayer shawl, the pockets hang down on either side and the contents will not fall out.

4. The pockets can be decorated with color crayons or pencils, with the design ironed after completion to make them waterproof. Waterproof pens can also be used. Any design conducive to healing and comfort can be used. If you know who the recipient will be, try to personalize the design for him or her. Choose words or scripture verses that will remind the person of God's love, or any positive thoughts that might be beneficial to this person.

5. The pockets can be used to hold prayers, cards, meaningful pieces of paper. We have found that when we give shawls to people, it is good to ask them if they have a special prayer request. Write the request on a card and put it in the pocket. For some reason, concerns come up for these prayer cards that have not been expressed in regular conversation.

Many blessings on your fabric prayer-shawl crafting!

—*Judith Pruess-Mellow*

The Meaning of Colors

The following lists some common associations made with particular colors. These associations may be helpful to you if you have a particular intention for your craft that you want to support with color:

Red:	Confidence, courage, vitality
Brown:	Earth, order
Orange:	Vitality with endurance
Pink:	Love, beauty
Green:	Life, fertility, well-being
Purple:	Spirituality, royalty
Blue:	Truth, peace
Gold:	Prosperity, wisdom
Yellow:	Happiness, intellectual energy
Indigo:	Intuition, meditation
White:	Purity, cleansing
Gray:	Maturity, security
Black:	Stability, mystery

Looking at Patterns

"I am not a 'religious' person, whatever that means, but I consider myself a spiritual person. I am also an avid craftsperson. I do a lot of knitting and quilting to give away. Last week I knit a hat for a friend's daughter. She just turned fourteen and is going through chemotherapy for a very aggressive form of thyroid cancer. As I knit her hat, I thought about her and the people who love her. I thought about the chemicals moving through her body and imagined them finding and eliminating the cancer cells. I imagined her losing her gorgeous hair and having it regrow even more beautiful than before, and envisioned her as a healthy young adult. When I left it at her door for her, I wrote a note to let her know that love and hope were knit into every stitch and that I hoped she would feel it as she wore it.

"I also knit hats and scarves for foster children and also imagine them feeling loved, warm, and safe as they wear them.

"I learned to quilt when we lived in Taiwan and made quilts that were auctioned off to support orphanages there. I make quilts for an orphanage in Africa. The children there are AIDS orphans and the quilt is usually the first new thing they've received and often is their only possession. I love imagining the children as I piece squares together.

"I put some of myself in each thing I make and really enjoy the process more than the end result. It's meaningful to me to give myself to others in this way and I am happy to be an anonymous person sending love to someone else who, most often, I will never meet."

—DEDE NEILSON HELMSWORTH

AFFIRMATION BLANKETS

No matter how old we might be, there is something so comforting about being wrapped up in something soft and warm—as the cultural phenomenon known as a Snuggie (the TV-advertised blanket that you wear) demonstrated. Though we might not think of it as such, we all have some sort of "blankie," something that we pull out when we want to feel warm and comfortable, whether it's a favorite flannel shirt, a velour robe, or a crocheted throw.

Creating an affirmation blanket as a spiritual practice was inspired by a small, pink, fuzzy "blankie" that I bought for my daughter a number of years ago from the woman-owned company Affirmagy. On this blanket are printed the words that every child should travel through life knowing; they include "I am filled with unlimited possibilities," "I am held by loving hands," "I am a bright light in the world," and "I am a true miracle."

Though my daughter is now nine years old, she still sleeps with this; I have always been warmed by the thought that she can not only see but she can *feel* these words as they are in every way wrapped around her.

Our need for affirmative blankies doesn't go away with age; if anything, we perhaps need them more as we navigate a world that doesn't often stop to communicate what a bright light we are in it. Steward your own spiritual formation by noticing what words encourage you to get out from under that proverbial bushel, and let your light shine.

> "The artist has so much love to give back to the universe that it spills over, and the fallen drops become 'works of art.' It is love in another form."
>
> —NANCY JACKSON

Inner Inquiries for Journaling and Reflection

✳ What words will serve as your strength, your shield, at this time in your life?

✳ What words comfort you; what words do you need to wrap yourself up in right now—literally?

DIY: Crafting an Affirmation Blanket

Established quilters may be itching already to make an affirmation quilt instead of an affirmation blanket, and to do so, your quilting supplies and suppliers will inform you as to how best to proceed. You can also embroider your affirmation(s) on quilting squares, a pillowcase, or other lightweight fabric.

For those who would prefer to begin with a ready-made blanket that is then embellished, you'll find plenty of inexpensive fleece blankets to choose from (see the sidebar on what different colors mean in the "Prayer Shawls" section to guide you in choosing the color that will best support your particular affirmations), and then write your embel-

lishments on that blanket using fabric paint or fabric pens that won't wash off. You could end by sewing on appropriate charms, if desired.

Looking at Patterns

"Much has been written about knitting as a path to mindfulness, as a path to meditation, a way to slow down. There are many, many ways to meditate, and for myself, slowing the flow of thoughts is hard. I am not the kind of person who gets needles in hand and has an instant transcendental experience. Oh no, quite the opposite. I experience an opportunity for growth, is more like it.

"You see, those thoughts that come up aren't always 'Hmmmm...I wonder what I should make for dinner?' Those thoughts are easy to float away on their little disappearing word boat. No. The thoughts that come up are, 'Oh, that person really hurt me' or, 'Oh, did I really say that and will I ever be able to make it right?' or 'Oh, I really screwed up this time,' 'I will never get that time back,' 'I hurt,' 'I feel angry,' 'I feel the pain of that loss,' and of course, much more.

"I am not an expert at meditating and I don't know if I ever will be. But knitting can help me work through the concerns and thoughts and feelings about situations and problems. To that end, I brainstormed some possible focused thoughts to have during knitting—affirmations, if you will. Mantras, if you so choose. Meditation, if you are farther down the pike than I am! Ultimately, isn't that what meditation is about? Not just stilling the thoughts, but moving through them, with compassion and expansive connection, all the while bringing one closer to the Divine.

For blessing:
I feel grateful.
This is a thread of kindness and blessing.
May (wearer's name) feel my love.
I feel compassion.
I feel calm.
I bless this stitch.
May love flow from my heart to my hands to my stitches.
I feel part of the greater Good.
I bless this yarn, and these stitches.
I see beauty.
I feel centered.
May each stitch carry love and blessing.
I have boundless love.
I freely give of myself.

When thoughts come, and I revisit situations that bring up strong feelings for me, I have these affirmations to help:

I feel curious.
I feel calm.
I welcome my feelings.
With each stitch I am closer to healing.
I honor my experience.
This situation (person, event) *is a blessed part of the whole.*
I bless this stitch with my tears.
I am free to love.

And, when one is ready:

I release my fear/resentment/anger/doubt/judgment, etc., if only for this moment.

As feelings pass:

I feel grateful.
I feel loved.
I feel free.

What would you add to this list?"

—ANGELA MOBLEY

PRAYER CARDS

For those brought up in the Roman Catholic tradition, the craft of making prayer cards will no doubt bring back memories—these palm-sized color cards have been handed out for centuries (the oldest surviving prayer card is dated from 1423 and depicts St. Christopher). Imprinted with a religious image and often including a prayer or verse from Scripture, prayer cards have traditionally been passed out at important life events—confirmation, first communion, and even funerals, to remind those attending to pray for the deceased. Their small size makes them easy to carry—a pocket-sized card of comfort, especially for someone with a particular affinity to that saint.

But, especially with the recent advent of artist trading cards (known as ATCs) and accompanying supplies, making personalized prayer cards—prayer

> *Laborare est orare* [work is prayer].
> –TRADITIONAL SAYING

cards that depict images and words that speak directly to your heart's concerns—is easier than ever. When one of my spiritual directees brought in a lovely little prayer card that she had made, with an image of pine-green unmanicured wilderness and a quotation from D. H. Lawrence on it, I delighted in how she had made her prayer so portable, and so personal.

Whatever you are meditating on or praying for becomes the prayer card's content: you can do prayer cards for a particular person, using a color copy of a photograph of them; for a global concern, using headlines; or for your own heart's desire. You can write your own prayer, include a poem or quotation that is meaningful, or journal on it. You can even make a "deck" of prayer cards, with different prayer focuses on each one!

Inner Inquiries for Journaling and Reflection

* ❊ What are the deepest prayers of my heart right now?
* ❊ What (or who) do I want to be reminded of on a daily basis?
* ❊ What images best illustrate my prayer concern?
* ❊ What words add solace or dimension to my prayer?

DIY: Crafting a Prayer Card

The popularity of ATCs has led to a plethora of easily found supplies—you can buy precut cards in different colors and even find little envelopes to hold them. Some art-supply stores carry frames for displaying ATCs—you could keep current prayer concerns in a display by your personal altar or place where you pray. You can collage your prayer cards, paint them, draw or write on them, or all of the above! Experiment with the mediums that best reflect the prayers of your heart.

Guides for the Path

The following books will be helpful for exploring ways to expand this craft by creating a personalized deck of Tarot or divination cards:

Inspiration Tarot: A Workbook for Understanding and Creating Your Own Tarot Deck by Gail Fairfield and Patti Provo (Red Wheel/Weiser, 1991)

Soul Collage: An Intuitive Collage Process for Individuals and Groups by Seena B. Frost (Hanford Mead Publishers, 2001)

Looking at Patterns

"Spirituality and art are intertwined for me. I began exploring art practices in my teens. I was always drawn to the creative arts, but I struggled with meaning and content. I didn't know *what* to paint or draw. My early environments did not encourage right-brain experimentation (and its related failures and messiness). The left-brain reigned. Utilitarianism and logic insisted on a purpose for art, so I put my creative impulses to work professionally as a graphic designer. It was when I discovered women's spirituality in my twenties that I opened up artistically. Spirituality—in particular, the Goddess mysteries—gave me access to my intuitive faculties and permission to be perfectly imperfect. It also gave me meaningful content. I took inspiration from nature and from my experience as a woman, and rendered those energies into forms. I crafted magical talismans, and I painted.

"As my spirituality evolved, so did my art. The biggest shift I've noticed in my art is a movement away from the inner demand for recognizable forms and meaningful content. Art, like spiritual experience, has become much more of a process than the creation of a product or the arrival at a destination. In spiritual language, it's less about striving and more about being.

"One way this gets expressed through my art-as-spiritual-practice is using an altered book as a landing place for my soul. I start with a vintage book and I paint, draw, collage, and write—however I am moved. I am not attempting to make anything. I am just making. The altered book performs a similar function as a meditation cushion does for sitting practice. It's the place where the physical comes to rest as consciousness comes to center. The practice is similar to visual journaling. But, for me, journaling involves thinking and this practice, like sitting meditation, is about non-thinking. My hands do the work, allowing my mind to rest. At the end of a session, I also get to witness myself in the mirror of my creation.

"The gifts of using art as a spiritual practice are many: compassion, spaciousness, wholeness, permission, growth, integration, and learning. It is a means for pursuing that ancient edict: 'Know Thyself.'"

—ELKA EASTLY VERA

POWER POUCHES

I made mine at a Renaissance Fair that I attended with my family on one of my birthdays, and holding it now reminds me of the goals or hopes that I held for that new year. Cognac-colored, the leather is shiny and smooth, and the large African beads that I strung on the leather cord that closes it give a resounding clack—it is an abacus of my intentions; it is my power pouch.

Like the medicine bag of Native Americans, you can craft a power pouch (or prayer pouch) that holds *your* personal "medicine," the tiny reminders of things and qualities that help you to stand in your spiritual power. These could include a leaf, pebble, or bit of beach glass from a particular place that brings you solace; a small photograph of your loved ones; a scroll of spiritual wisdom; a representation of your particular faith path, such as a cross or Star of David; or any other minute memento that helps you to realign with what has the most heart and meaning for you…and with the Divine.

A variation of this could be a "magic bag." Once, when I was on a weekend camping trip—a Vision Quest—with a group of people, a friend gave me a magic bag before we separated to spend two days alone in nature. In it was a collection of whimsical things—a rainbow-colored birthday candle,

> "Creativity is so much more than art making. It is a tool for navigating through everyday experiences to find the sacred in each God-given moment."
>
> –KARLA M. KINCANNON

a dragonfly charm, a snip of gold-sequined fabric—but just sifting through its contents brought a smile to my face and a sense of the, yes, *magic* that can be found in everyday life.

Inner Inquiries for Journaling and Reflection

✳ What are my gifts, my talents, my wisdom? From where do I get my spiritual power, and what will best remind me of that?

✳ What helps me to remember my personal "medicine"?

✳ Have I lost my sense of life's "magic"? What could I carry that would remind me of it?

DIY: Crafting a Power Pouch

To make a power pouch, you will need a circle of leather or heavy fabric (approximately ten inches or less in diameter), a leather punch or hole punch, leather cord or satin cord to use as the drawstrings, and beads and other embellishments, if desired.

Punch holes approximately an inch apart around the edge of your circle. Thread your cord around that circle (going down through one hole and coming up through the next, until your cord has gone through all the holes). When done, make sure that the two ends of cord go up in the same direction (punch one final hole if necessary to make sure that the two cord ends both can be pulled from the outside of the bag). String beads on each cord, if desired—then knot the two cord ends together tightly. Pulling on the cords should draw the material together, making a pouch.

"The most beautiful thing we can experience is the mysterious."

—ALBERT EINSTEIN

CRAFTING FOR CONTEMPLATION

Chapter 4:

CRAFTING FOR CONTEMPLATION

> "An essential portion of any artist's labor is not creation so much as invocation. Part of the work cannot be made, it must be received; and we cannot have this gift except, perhaps, by supplication, by courting, by creating within ourselves that 'begging bowl' to which the gift is drawn."
> —RODERICK MACIVER

A FAMOUS SPIRITUAL TEACHER WAS SPEAKING TO A LARGE audience of mostly young people on the subject of meditation, so the older woman sitting right in the front row really stood out. He noticed that she smiled and nodded through most of the talk, so after he was finished he sought her out. "I see you already are familiar with many of the benefits of regular meditation," he said. "Well," she said, smiling at him indulgently, "I do crochet, you know."

This anecdote may be apocryphal but it speaks to the meditative effects that immersing ourselves in a craft can have. As mystic Evelyn Underhill wrote, "All artists are of necessity in some measure contemplative"—and if you're reading this book you know that to be true, or soon will.

Most of the crafts in this chapter—prayer mats, tray sand gardens, luminarias, rock cairns, and meditation cushions—have their origins in Eastern religious traditions (and interestingly, all of them come from other cultures). There is a simplicity to each of them, and an elegance: One's focus in these crafts is narrowed to a single point: a defined ground, a rock, a flame.

The practice perhaps lies less in the making and more in the using of them, during which our "begging bowl"—as Roderick MacIver referred to it in the quotation that opens this chapter—is filled up yet again.

"The sacred creative cycle has two arcs. The descending arc is external. It is the work of our hands as we manifest spirit in material form. The ascending arc is internal. It is the journey for inspiration and direct contact with spirit. Both are necessary, and both can lead us into art as a spiritual practice."

—TOM CROCKETT

PRAYER MATS

Who growing up *wasn't* enchanted by stories of magic carpets, fringed flying rugs that whisked you from one exotic place to another? While we may not think of it as "magic," having a special place—a holy ground—designated for the sacred time spent in prayer and meditation can also help us to escape one world (our daily everyday lives) and be transported to another (the very presence of God). For some that might be an entire room. For others, it might just be a chair and table in the corner, or a garden bench outside. Whether you have a specific place in which you pray—or if you are challenged in finding space you can call your own—a prayer mat can help you to define that space; it can even create that space on its own.

Additionally, a prayer mat can help you with focusing your attention back on your prayer or meditation; in one Muslim practice, particular points on a prayer mat are used as a gentle reminder to refocus. When crafting a prayer mat as a spiritual practice, you could consciously include such reminders. You could also approach your prayer mat as a metaphor: On what does your faith stand? Incorporate words or an image that portray what "lies beneath" your sense of Spirit.

> "The act of painting is a spiritual covenant between the maker and the higher powers. The intent of the artist flows through the work of art, no matter what the technique or style."
> —AUDREY FLACK

Whether you choose to buy an existing mat and embellish it to make it your own, or craft one yourself, creating a prayer mat—which literally can become your Ground of Being—is a powerful practice both in the crafting and in the using of it.

Inner Inquiries for Journaling and Reflection

✳ Do I have a special defined area in which I pray and meditate? If not, how and where could I create one?

✳ What symbols and colors best represent to me the leaving behind of the workaday world and being transported to the Most Holy?

DIY: Crafting a Prayer Mat

Basic materials for making a prayer mat include heavy canvas (many craft stores carry pre-primed canvas floor cloth in different sizes), flat exterior paint, latex or acrylic paints, stencils and rubber stamps, paintbrushes, and a lead pencil to trace your design.

The first step is to prepare the canvas—even if it's been primed, brush a coat of flat exterior paint on it, and straighten the edges after it's dried (cut a half-inch of material along all four sides, then measure another half-inch from the edge of the cloth on all four sides again). Fold the canvas against this line, and stitch in place with a sewing machine. Onto this, paint another coat of the background color.

Once it's dry, you can begin to apply your design, which could be a labyrinth, a mandala, a sacred symbol, or a verse from your Scriptures. You can use stencils and stamps, too. If you're working with an intricate design, use the lead pencil to draw it onto your prayer mat (you can also tape your mat to the wall and, using an overhead projector, project an image on to it to trace). Use painter's tape as needed to keep colors from blurring into each other. Another tip to keep color from smearing is to only work on one area of the mat at a time, and letting it dry before starting the next one. You can use a hairdryer to make the paint dry faster.

After your design is finished and completely dry, remove any residue from the surface with a damp sponge. Then apply polyurethane with a clean brush, using long and consistent strokes, to preserve your pattern (two or even three coats work best, allowing it to dry completely between coats).

TRAY SAND GARDENS

"Zen...shows us that all things are perfect and complete, just as they are. Nothing is lacking. In trying to realize our true nature, we rub against the same paradox: We don't know that we already are what we are trying to become... It's the same with art. Each one of us is already an artist, whether we realize it or not... Engaging the creative process is a way of getting in touch with this truth, and to let it function in all areas of our lives."

–JOHN DAIDO LOORI

When I first saw the famous Ryoanji Temple garden in Kyoto, famous for its placement of black rocks on white pebbles, I found myself mesmerized by its simplicity and grace—something no photograph of it can fully convey. Millions before me have had the same experience—and there have been academic papers written to analyze this response. According to one of these, the particular pattern of the rocks leaves a subconscious impression of a tree, and the sensitivity of our subconscious minds to the artful associations between the rocks may be why the garden is so calming. Perhaps that explains the haiku that I felt inspired to write before leaving the temple grounds?

Unlike Western gardens, which can bombard viewers with their pluralistic and profuse beauty, a Zen rock garden is a minimalist meditation: a few rocks, a lawn of smaller pebbles, a raked design. It is deceiving in its simplicity, profound in its execution. There is nothing there that is not supposed to be there…but what is there will be experienced differently by everyone—and even by you, if you take the time to view it from different perspectives.

Trying to understand Zen art and craft is fruitless without an understanding of the culture it comes from. This awareness came to me on another trip to another place: Standing atop Uluru (formerly called Ayers Rock) in the heart of the Australian desert, and seeing the same scrubby dots of dry bush below me that are reflected in the pointillistic dots of Aborigine art, I realized how the art native to a country often reflects that country's landscape and culture. Thus, I understood the haunting beauty of a Zen rock garden after spending a bit of time in Japan; it reveals a disciplined impulse that is diametrically opposed to our Western excess—and for that reason alone, a tray sand garden can be a useful form of meditation. Just like life!

> "Art although produced by man's hands, is something not created by hands alone, but something which wells up from a deeper source out of our soul."
>
> —VINCENT VAN GOGH

Inner Inquiries for Journaling and Reflection

⁎ Is there any excess in my life right now?

⁎ What do I need to prune, to eliminate?

⁎ What do I need to arrange—what needs better "placement" in my life?

⁎ What will help my energy to flow more easily and fully?

DIY: Crafting a Tray Sand Garden

To make your own tray sand garden, find or make a shallow wooden box in a dimension that intrigues you (most tray sand gardens are rectangular, but do not feel bound by this shape). Consider keeping colors minimal; there is something very arresting about black rocks on white sand. Fill your tray with sand, and place rocks on top of the sand—your meditation will begin with the very placement of the elements. Zen gardens are raked; you can use a doll's rake or even use a wide-toothed comb to make patterns in the sand. Let your inner Observer bear witness to what thoughts and feelings come up as you work with your tray sand garden— and consider employing haiku into this practice if desired.

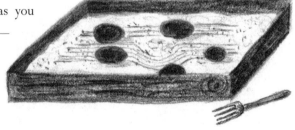

Flashes of Inspiration

"I keep a magic wishing box on my desk. Every so often, I look at it and make a wish upon my heart's desire. It can be made of a bowl or lidless box, filled halfway with sand. The wish stones are placed in the sand in any arrangement that is pleasing: agate for a new home, amethyst for spirituality, carnelian or lapis lazuli for a job, coral for wanting children, fool's gold for money, and rose quartz for love."

—BRENDA KNIGHT

L U M I N A R I A S

It was on a visit to Santa Fe—a road-trip pilgrimage made with my mother to Arizona and New Mexico to visit the sleepy "hotbeds" of Navajo folk artists—that I first experienced the luminous magic of *luminarias*, the traditional Mexican lanterns made from ornately cut brown-paper bags with candles lit inside. How enchanting it is, to see so many of them, lined up in rows—and what a wonderful symbol they are, of the beautiful light that we each hold inside. The tradition of making *luminarias* comes from Catholicism; placing them outside the home during Christmastime symbolizes an act of hope that the spirit of the Christ child would be guided to one's home.

And holding that as a framework can make the creating of *luminarias* more meaningful. To think of them as lights along the path—the spiritual path—begs contemplation of those people, places, and things that have been lights on *our* paths.

Thus the craft of making *luminarias* can be a celebration in any season that we honor our spiritual "lights"—those who have lit the way before us. And whether you choose to create *luminarias* from paper that will later be discarded or make coverings for glass votive candleholders to keep

"One way to feed our souls is through the creative process. Learning about our soul or spirit or inner self is like looking up a gently spiraling stair. There is always something more, something new just around the curve, just out of sight. A ray of light might illuminate one spot while the step beyond waits in darkness. Does the flight end? Continue upward? Is there a door? Is it open? Closed? The only way to find out is to climb the stair."

—JANET CARIJA BRANDT

up year-round, spending time honoring that which has brought you light is a significant spiritual practice indeed.

Inner Inquiries for Journaling and Reflection

* Who are the ancestors, teachers, or other influences that have lit the way before me?

* Who shines their light in my life right now?

* Have I expressed my gratitude for these lights? Have I expressed my gratitude to those people whose lights have guided me?

DIY: Crafting a Luminaria

Luminarias are simple to make, and a wonderful craft to do with children. Basically, they're paper bags that have been cut through with tiny shapes, weighted down with sand, and have a votive candle inside—the light from the candle is seen through the delicate shapes that have been cut into the bag.

They are traditionally used to light paths, though you can also place them on a mantel or table. Use bags made of colored paper, or embellish them yourself. One caveat: Keep your shapes small in size—no more than an inch or an inch-and-a-half, because the bigger they are, the more wind they can let in—which will blow your candle out—and the more likely they are to tear or lose their shape. You can use small cookie cutters or punches with holes in a shape. (If you love the idea of bigger shapes, then try inserting a colored paper bag inside the bag cut with larger shapes; the inner bag will serve as both a liner and as color decoration.) Fill your *luminaria* with an inch or two of sand in the bottom, and nestle a votive candle or tealight in the center.

This little light of mine
I'm gonna let it shine
This little light of mine
I'm gonna let it shine
This little light of mine
I'm gonna let it shine
Let it shine, let it shine,
Let it shine!

—TRADITIONAL

ROCK CAIRNS

There is a certain mysterious quality to rock cairns, which stand as small Stonehenges—arresting yet inscrutable. They have been made for thousands of years, as altars, as focuses for meditation and prayer, as symbols of hope, and as pointers to the way home. Cairns are each unique, like snowflakes; but what they share in common is material (rock) and form (rocks stacked on top of each other).

Modern-day artists are working with rock cairns, building these mysterious towers which carry different meanings for each viewer. They are, literally, a practice—for with any misplacement, the cairn will come tumbling down. For that reason, concentration is vitally important—making rock cairns is truly a method for cultivating present-moment awareness.

> "Direct spiritual experience gives us the conviction that we are natural residents of the realm of the Beyond and the Whole, that we are loved and created to love, that it is our nature to be creative. From such direct experience, great quantities of energy are released in the world."
> —THOMAS RYAN

If you feel drawn to exploring rock cairns as a spiritual practice, you can work on as large a scale as you want—using stones as light or as heavy as you can handle. Possibilities include stacking small stones from a treasured collection as a morning meditation; actually crafting and affixing stones together to "point the way home"; or creating cairns outdoors, which will offer different reflections with the changing seasons. However you choose to explore the craft of rock-cairn making, you will find that it is a practice that will never be "set in stone."

Inner Inquiries for Journaling and Reflection

✳ What feels "stacked up" in my life right now?

✳ What has top priority in my life—and what can be left for later?

✳ What is the foundation on which I balance my life?

Looking at Patterns

"During a tour of the Holy Land, I visited the church on the traditional site of Jesus's miracle of multiplication of the loaves and the fish. In the gift shop, there were stones gathered from the shore of the Sea of Galilee with the sign of a fish stamped on them. I immediately purchased some. I've always collected rocks, whether at the beach or in the mountains. I decided it was time to use them in a spiritual practice.

"On my home altar, I now have a circle of the 'fish' stones and a row of other stones. As I start my morning intercessory prayers, I gather up the stones. As I reset the circle, I dedicate each stone to a concern. I might be praying for someone who is ill. I might be asking for blessings on a project. I might be praying for peace in an area of the world. Every day the prayers are different, and I try to remember those concerns whenever I see that circle during the day.

"My row of stones includes one in the shape of an island I love, another that looks like a Madonna that reminds me to honor the Sacred Feminine, and another that has a gaping mouth that I call my 'Prophet' stone. I have some others that are stamped with reminders: Teach, Organize, Balance. Placing them on my altar is a way of refreshing those intentions. I also keep one stone that I call 'the stone.' It doesn't have to be anything other than a gift from the Earth."

—MARY ANN BRUSSAT

"Once you love an art enough that you can be taken up in it, you are able to experience an echo of the great creative act that mysteriously has given life to us all. It may be the closest any of us can get to God."

—KENT NERBURN

MEDITATION CUSHIONS

Like a prayer mat, a meditation cushion (often referred to as a "zafu"), defines sacred space—it is literally a place on which we can sit, inviting us out of our day-to-day activities into the deeper aspects of existence: time spent in the presence of God.

Zafus, the traditional Buddhist meditation cushions that rise higher from the floor in order to give practitioners of sitting meditation a straighter (and often more comfortable) posture, are made of two same-sized circular fabric pieces, separated by a long rectangular piece that is gathered and sewn around the circumference. They are usually filled

> "Whether your medium be music, watercolors, clay, gardening, woodworking, cooking, dance, or voice, the Creator has gifted you with creativity. Your gift in return is to use it."
>
> –THOMAS RYAN

with buckwheat or flaxseed, which provides a firm but flexible cushion. If you are not interested in making a cushion for meditation but rather contemplation, then you have more shapes and materials to choose from. Spend time reflecting on how this craft will best support your spiritual practice.

Author and philosopher Alan Watts once said this about meditation: "We could say that meditation doesn't have a reason or doesn't have a purpose. In this respect it's unlike almost all other things we do except perhaps making music and dancing. When we make music we don't do it in order to reach a certain point... Also, when we are dancing we are not aiming to arrive at a particular place on the floor as in a journey... And exactly the same thing is true in meditation. Meditation is the discovery that the point of life is always arrived at in the immediate moment."

Watts' words could also be used about making a meditation cushion; because while there is an end point—a completed cushion—like many of the other crafts explored here, the making of your meditation cushion will play less of a part in your spiritual practice than the actual use of it will. Find fabrics and a form that will inspire you to *sit*...in the Silence.

Inner Inquiries for Journaling and Reflection

* What can I place into my life that will encourage me to sit...in the Silence?

* What will best support my meditation efforts? (What time of day? What type of meditation? For how long?)

* What prevents me from keeping a regular meditation practice? What might I do to change that?

DIY: Crafting a Meditation Cushion

More experienced sewers who practice sitting meditation might want to craft a zafu. If that's something that calls to you, you can find easy instructions at finecraftguild.com/how-to-zafu-meditation-pillow/.

You might also just explore making a simple cushion, made from two large squares of fabric sewn together on all sides and filled with seeds or batting. If you use muslin, you could approach this like your prayer shawl—by using fabric pens or paints (or crayons and colored pencils that are later ironed to preserve them) to write verses or quotations on the surface of the cushion that will remind you of the reasons it's important to create the time to meditate.

Looking at Patterns

"I started learning how to meditate when I was about thirty-two. I had dabbled in it several times before, but my regular practice started in my early thirties. A couple of times when I was sewing I noticed that I was getting better results in clearing my mind/meditating than when I was actually meditating. From then on I have consciously used crafting as a way of attaining peace.

"To anyone who wants to use their crafting as a spiritual practice, I would advise keeping things simple, to give yourself blank space in your thoughts so that your mind can rest. The following are suggestions for how to do that:

1) *Simplify your projects.* You can start with sewing; the most basic tools for sewing are a needle and a thread. They can be found anywhere, even in the first-aid kit in an office. Your cloth can be an old shirt or an old sweater you wash in the washing machine with hot water, to felt. Some embroidery floss at twenty-five cents a bundle will be great to have too, and scissors. That's all. It will give you beautiful results. Your first pieces could be what you need for a basic sewing kit, like a needle book, a pincushion, a scissor holder, and so on.

2) *Simplify your tools and materials.* Make things from what you already have. Many people start crafting so they can have joy and peace of mind, but soon find themselves driving around town, shopping in the mall, surfing on the Internet, and a whole day is gone and nothing has been made—the goal has not been attained.

3) *Simplify your environment.* Start with small projects that you can carry on a bus or a train, or keep in your purse to do at lunchtime whether at your desk or on a nearby park bench. Simplify the sounds around you, and the visual clutter. If you can, stay with your handwork and just do that, with no music, phone conversations, or television on. It's okay to have people around you or to be in a public place. Soon you'll be immersed in the project and you'll tune them out.

4) *Start with an intention.* Keep yourself or the person you are making the item for in mind, and also your intention for that person. You could be knitting a prayer shawl for a friend who has cancer, or making a guardian doll for a child that cannot go to sleep at night, or sewing a pair of oven mittens for yourself. The intention is important, and acts as a prayer. No matter how ordinary your piece might seem to you, the spiritual results are always extraordinary and touch the heart of both the maker and the receiver."

—PARDIS AMIRSHAHI

"Know the nature of creating.
Where there is joy, there is creating.
Know the nature of joy.
Where there is the Infinite, there is joy."

—*THE UPANISHADS*

CRAFTING FOR CREATION

Chapter 5:

CRAFTING FOR CREATION

"The important thing is that creation is God's, and that we are part of it,
and being part of creation is for us to be cocreators with [God] in the
continuing joy of new creation."
–MADELEINE L'ENGLE

EACH CRAFT WE MAKE IS, OF COURSE, A NEW CREATION—
something that did not exist before we gathered our tools and pieced it into being. But
we can take that further—indeed, not only every craft we make but every day we make
is a new creation. We are always in a state of some sort of creation with every choice we
make—from how to best complete a work project to what to make for dinner.

Seeing our creativity more broadly—that we are always in the process of creating
something, from the mundane to the magnificent—can give us greater freedom in
embracing our own creativity. Then, it is not what a few of the exalted are; it is what we
all are—creative beings.

And when we consciously create a work of art, we more deeply understand how we are also crafting our very lives. As Catherine Moon writes, "The act of creating empowers us to have a say in how we will shape and respond to the suffering and hope within us. By creating art we participate in the creation of ourselves."

"Use whatever talents you possess. The woods would be very silent if no birds sang there except the very best."
—HENRY VAN DYKE

In these deeper, more conscious creative attempts, most people report a sense of grace, of dancing with the Mystery. In a lovely poem called "Collaboration," English professor Alan Nordstrom gives a sense of this creative collaboration with the ineffable:

Here in this sanctuary of the night
I wake and rise, then sit, compose and write,
For only here and now may I draw near
That secret solitude where thoughts appear.

The night is still, my mind grows keenly calm,
The fragrance of the tea I sip's a balm
Wafting me to a height of consciousness
Where sound and sense and image coalesce.

This spell I enter lasts an hour or two,
A rapture out of which comes something new
Produced by fusing intellect with air,
The stuff of thought inspired, refined, made rare.

I cannot help but feel that self and soul
Collaborate to shape what here is whole.

In this chapter you will discover prayer paintings, intention jewelry, inner wisdom dolls, icons, and messages in a bottle—all crafts that will tap into that inner pool of guidance, wisdom, and personal symbology that is uniquely yours. As you explore them, may your self and soul—to use Alan's words—collaborate, to shape what is Whole.

PRAYER PAINTINGS

As I enter the darkened studio, I want to weep; the sheer aesthetic beauty of what is before me brings tears to my eyes. There is a table containing a profusion of pastries, fruits, nuts, and seeds on colorful pottery plates, delicious both to eat and to drink in visually—it speaks to generosity, the generosity of our hostess and of nature. In the background are the haunting yet beautiful strains of a Gregorian chant, wrapping us all in blankets of sacred notes. And at each place of the three art tables, set up in a "U" shape at the back of the room, a spiritual tableau has been set: in front of everyone is a lit candle of the Virgin of Guadalupe; a container of clear water to dip brushes into; colored markers; a notecard and envelope, on which to write our intentions for the day...and sequins, a heap of vibrantly colored sequins—because, above all, this is to be a celebration.

This is part of what I wrote on my notecard, what my heart told me in that moment: "Slow down...rest...soak in sacredness, art, color, and solitude. The blend of spirituality and creativity is my deepest inner passion... 'Feed your heart and your soul with all that you love' is the message..."

I had just entered the world of Shiloh Sophia McCloud, who, in addition to creating prayer paintings herself (she has her own gallery in Healdsburg, California, and has been showing her work professionally for almost two decades), also

> "The creation story is not something God does or did. It is what God *is*. It is a process within the Principle acting on itself. Creativity is the God process in you, expressing as you. The creation is your story, the key to your creative genius."
>
> —ERIC BUTTERWORTH

has a mission to help women bring forth their inner guidance, and guides, on canvas.

As Shiloh describes on one of her websites, "Painting for me is a devotional act, a spiritual practice, a prayer, and a way to share my love. My creations are the bountiful harvest from a life lived in service to Beauty and the Divine... My creations are both my offering and my overflow.

"When I create with inquiry and intention, I am able to open a door to the sacred space between worlds. That is where I paint from—straddling spirit and matter, unmanifest and manifest, broken dreams and dreams fulfilled, suffering and healing. It is here that I find I can synchronize my own heartbeat with that of the world. Where I am in some small way one with all that is, even just for a few moments."

In that last sentence, Shiloh has encapsulated the sacred kernel at the heart of crafting as a spiritual practice—that through it, we can become one with all that is...and with All That Is. Through creating our own prayer paintings, we can do the same.

"I call the form of painting I do intuitive painting," Shiloh explains. "It's accessing the images and symbols from the unconscious; not looking to nature as your reference for the sourcing of your content. When the image is drawn from within, there's nothing to compare it to—that's why it can be such a tool for reflection, because it yields up something unexpected, something I didn't know before." It also, Shiloh points out, eliminates our unhelpful tendency to compare our artwork with others: "It is a discipline to not allow the [inner] Critic to show up in the way of your freedom... the Muse is the counterpoint of the Critic; when we listen to her as the primary voice, then the Critic shapeshifts into a discerning voice"—and something constructive.

Shiloh has created a DVD set that can guide people through the process (see "Guides for the Path" on the following page), but there are additional ways to approach painting as a prayer. One woman I know woke up every morning and painted the simple image of an empty bowl as a reminder to clear herself of any expectations of what the day might hold and to be open and receptive to what she might encounter during that day.

One might also conclude the day with a simple watercolor wash of colors, shapes, and patterns that represent the experience of the previous sixteen hours. Notice what size you feel drawn to working with (small sketchbook or large canvas?), as well as what material calls to you (thick oils, opaque acrylics, transparent watercolors? What might that medium have to say about your life right now?).

Find the format that best supports your intention from the practice, and see what reveals itself—for it may lead to an understanding about your very purpose in life. As Shiloh says, "A creative spiritual practice is part of what grants you access to answering your calling. It's almost impossible to answer your calling without some form of creativity. Access that calling within yourself—into that calling which is uniquely yours to express."

Inner Inquiries for Journaling and Reflection

* How do I want to use this craft—as a daily meditation? For the exploration of conscious or unconscious personal symbols? As a release...or as catalyst?

* Do I know my calling in life? What does painting reveal to me about that?

Guides for the Path

If you are interested in exploring painting as a spiritual practice, check out Shiloh's DVD set, "Our Lady of the Divine Spark," which will take you through the process. You can find information about that and her other creative endeavors at www.shilohsophia.com.

You might also investigate the work of Michele Cassou, the innovator of "The Painting Experience," a process by which people, through paint, tap into their creative expression (thepaintingexperience.com); and explore the book by Linda Novick, *The Painting Path: Embodying Spiritual Discovery Through Yoga, Brush and Color* (Skylight Paths, 2007).

Crafting a Spiritual Practice

"The most important thing in crafting as a spiritual practice is the commitment—it really doesn't happen without it. And the commitment is often inconvenient and uncomfortable in the beginning, until you've become dependent on that commitment to enjoy your days.

"So I make an agreement with myself to create every day, in some way—whether that's painting or writing or whatever. For someone just getting started, I would suggest two things:

1. A dedicated time section that you commit to every day, whether it's for five minutes or twenty-two minutes or a half-hour—a commitment that within a twenty-four-hour segment you will create for that specified amount of time; and if nothing comes, you'll just sit there. This trains your body, mind, and spirit to receive a download.

2. In terms of approach, it's a perception shift to view everything that you're doing as sacred. In the words of my mentor, Sue Hoya Sellars, 'Make the mundane sacred.'"

—SHILOH MCCLOUD

INTENTION JEWELRY

Of all the creative spiritual practices in this book, intention jewelry is perhaps the closest one to my heart, because it serves so well and so immediately to remind me of that which I want always to remember: that I am spiritual being having a human experience, not the other way around…or, as a dearly regarded teacher used to say, it reminds me with just a glance downward who—and Whose—I am.

In 2002, a book I co-wrote on prayer beads—*A String and a Prayer: How to Make and Use Prayer Beads*—was published, and I have continued to make prayer (or "intention") jewelry in the decade since. But I realize that this idea of using jewelry as a way of keeping my dreams and intentions before

> "The very act of creating something beautiful is God in action through your own two hands."
>
> —SONIA CHOQUETTE

me has been a part of my life for many years before that. Think about it: Have you ever worn a religious symbol, a charm that you got on vacation, or a piece of jewelry made by your child? Though we might not call them "intention" jewelry, pieces such as that do carry our intentions—to follow our faith, to remember a treasured place, to honor our beloved son or daughter.

When I sift through the box where I keep my prayer beads, the strands I have made for particular intentions, I am delighted by the diversity I see: a black-and-white beaded cuff made from memory wire, spelling out in tiny alphabet beads my statement of life purpose; a strand I made to reflect on my marriage, using beads intentionally to mark particular points for contemplation (for example, the bead made from cloudy recycled Coke-bottle glass invites me to ask, What issues, thoughts, habits am I recycling—unproductively—into this relationship? A square bead, clear as water, invites the reflection, Where am I transparent in my relationship? Where am I not?); a long "shawl" prayer strand, made for my ordination as an interfaith minister to wear with my stole, containing beads from around the world and sacred images from different cultures and creeds. Affixed at the bottom is a sterling-silver cylinder, set with garnets, containing a tiny rolled-up scroll on which I've printed my personal vows of ministry.

Making a bracelet, necklace, or simple beaded strand to hang from a keychain that supports our most deeply held intentions is an empowering spiritual practice, because it literally keeps that sacred desire before us. Why not create an intention strand that validates you as a creative being? As Julia Cameron suggests in *Finding Water*, "Art is a language of symbols. Gift yourself with a symbolic something that speaks to you of your identity as an artist… There are as many symbols of creativity as there are forms of creativity. Select the symbol that speaks most clearly to your heart."

There are many wonderful books available on symbols, which will give you historical, cultural, and folkloric references for what particular symbols mean. One of the best is *The Book of Symbols: Reflections on Archetypal Images*, edited by Ami Ronnberg and Kathleen Martin, and filled with color images from The Archive for Research in Archetypal Symbolism (Taschen, 2010). When contemplating intention jewelry, ask yourself what would best support the purpose for making it—visual symbols, such as charms; natural objects, such as shells or seeds; actual words, which could be spelled out with alphabet beads? And depending on your answers to those questions, what format would best suit the materials and best suit your practice: a necklace that you wear in ceremony? a bracelet that you wear every day? a strand that you keep in your pocket or purse, or on your keychain?

However you answer those questions, you will find intention jewelry to be visual anchors, a daily reminder, of all that you hope to be and become. To paraphrase Gandhi, "bead" the change you wish to see in the world!

Inner Inquiries for Journaling and Reflection

* What is my most deeply held intention right now? Is it general (for example, "spend more time in prayer") or specific ("eat more healthfully")?

* Do I have more than one deeply held intention at this point in my life? If so, what is a symbol or key word for each of those intentions? How can I remind myself of them?

Guides for the Path

The following resources may be helpful to you as you explore making intention jewelry as a spiritual practice:

A String and a Prayer: How to Make and Use Prayer Beads by Eleanor Wiley and Maggie Oman Shannon (Red Wheel/Weiser, 2002)

A String of Expression: Techniques for Transforming Art and Life into Jewelry by June Roman (North Light Books, 2010)

Inspiritu Jewelry: Earrings, Bracelets, and Necklaces for the Mind, Body, and Spirit by Marie French (North Light Books, 2011)

Looking at Patterns

"I offer workshops on making personal prayer beads. The finished beads are like fingerprints—I've never seen any two alike. I supply the beads, string, and other supplies, but I ask folks to bring a bead or a button...anything we can string that has meaning for them (a bead from Grandmother's broken necklace, a button from the wornout flannel shirt that Dad wore every Saturday of his life).

"We set our intention for the beads before we make our selection from the tables filled with beads. Some people choose beads to represent the many things they are grateful for; others choose beads that remind them of the important people in their lives who they want to pray for. The possibilities are endless: prayers for the planet, prayers for peace, etc. After everyone has tied a tassel to the end of their prayer beads, we hold them to our hearts and bless them. It has been so heartwarming to see people with their prayer beads in hand some eight to ten years after they made them in a workshop. They become a part of us and remind us that prayer, and praying one bead at a time, is a deep spiritual practice.

"I often make beads from clay for the workshops. This is a special spiritual practice for me in preparation for the workshops. When I travel I pick up beads, shells, and seeds that can be strung. People love to know they have something in their prayer beads from a foreign place like a beach in Morocco or shells from the Caribbean."

–CLAIRE L. JAGEMANN

Inner Wisdom Dolls

I was one of those little girls who loved dolls, and I had many while growing up. I am only a few months older than the Barbie doll—which was officially introduced to the world in the spring of 1959—and my first kindergarten picture shows me standing outside the elementary school, clutching my tow-headed Barbie in her emerald-

> "I believe that what doesn't get through to us in words may get through to us in images; some things in our lives are 'too deep for words,' but not necessarily for images."
>
> —CHARLES MCCOLLOUGH

green satin suit. Dolls helped to expand my creativity and my understanding of the world; a voracious and precocious reader, I would act out scenes from the novels I read with my dolls (employing my little brother's G. I. Joes when necessary). More educational than that, however, were the wonderful, and wonderfully diverse, dolls that my grandmother bought me on her travels around the world: an apple-cheeked granny with apron and tiny straw basket from Ireland; a cappuccino-colored beauty with black-lace mantilla from Spain; a tiny silk couple seated on a half-moon made of bamboo stalk from Japan. Through them (some of which I still have, to pass on to my own daughter), I got glimpses of spiritual energy, the energy of the cultures and the people being represented.

And though doll-making is not one of my primary creative practices, the two dolls that I have made through the years have had profound lessons to teach me and continue to inform me still, which is why they both hold places of honor on a home-office bookshelf.

My doll-making debut occurred one evening after spending time outside earlier that afternoon, in a meditation that offered powerful insights. At a time in my life when I was burning the candle at both ends—juggling a job with graduate school, the care of my then-three-year-old with caregiving to my ailing mother, and working on my fifth book in my "leisure time"—I felt seriously burnt-out. It was then that the apple tree directly in front of my gaze spoke to me—spoke to me of the cycles of nature and the seasons, reminding me that even an apple tree doesn't bear fruit *constantly.*

That night, I made my first doll, having found in a bin of art supplies a true-to-scale plastic apple, which—with its inner core scraped out and placed on the neck of an empty plastic water bottle—composes the head of my inner wisdom doll. With glued-on yarn hair, tree branches for arms, and a fabric shift that covers her transparent "body," she reminds me to be attentive to natural cycles, to allow myself to rest, to not expect myself to bear fruit constantly. Though my schedule hasn't changed much, remaining still as full as ever, my attitudes have. I try to relax more often, allow myself space to rest, reflect, rejuvenate.

My second doll carries a different energy; she serves more as a totem or representation of my inner wisdom. Crafted similarly to a bundle of sage, this fabric Sage reminds me to keep things in perspective. Her wizened face—prefabricated in clay—reminds me of the span of time, that things that seem so important today will not be important when I am her age.

Wrapping cotton batting around a stick to fashion her body, then wrapping fabric around that to fashion her robe, and ribbon around the fabric to hold the "clothes" on tight, this doll is self-contained. Her robe is a batik of turquoise, lavender, midnight blue;

her breasts are two discs with tiny star-shaped holes; her hair is Medusa-like threads of wool and ribbon; and the charms that adorn her include a star, an open hand, the word "wisdom," a dragonfly. She is a scepter that I can hold when I need to remind myself of my innate wisdom, the wisdom of the ages that lies within us all.

Inner Inquiries for Journaling and Reflection

* ✳ How connected do I feel right now to my inner wisdom?
* ✳ What aspects of my life do I need guidance on right now?
* ✳ In my meditations or prayers, have I received any important messages? Any important images or words?

DIY: Crafting an Inner Wisdom Doll

After contemplating the questions above, notice if there are any compelling symbols that will influence the doll you want to make (as my apple-tree meditation resulted in my apple-head doll).

To make a simple doll, find an empty plastic water bottle and affix something on the top for its head—this could be a Styrofoam ball or other material, such as my cored plastic apple. If you want to include arms (mine were twigs), affix them to the plastic bottle using duct or another strong tape. Fabric will cover a multitude of crafting sins— you can drape a thin muslin piece over a Styrofoam head and paint a face on it (attach it by rubber band around the neck of the bottle, then cover the rubber band with a beaded "choker" that you make), and also hide your taped-on arms by wrapping fabric around them to make your doll's sleeves.

Should this become a crafting practice that you want to refine, a good source to explore is *Soul Mate Dolls: Dollmaking as a Healing Art* by Noreen Crone-Findlay (Krause Publications, 2000). In that book, the author includes actual patterns that you can use to make your own inner wisdom dolls.

ICONS

In a San Francisco neighborhood near mine, there is a tucked-away treasure called the Archangel Bookstore, which carries Orthodox Christian books, worship supplies, and icons. It was there that I bought the one that I've contemplated for years; as small as my palm, it is a depiction of Mary and her baby Jesus, their faces silhouetted by carved silver.

Reflecting on an icon is a spiritual devotion that has been practiced for thousands of years; the first icon painter is believed to have been the apostle Paul, whose subject was Mary. As icon painting evolved, prayer was considered to be integral to the practice—taking place in the artist's preparation before the icon was painted, during the actual painting process, and by the observer when contemplating the completed painting.

There has been a quiet resurgence of interest in working with icons as a spiritual practice; one modern book, *Praying with Icons* by Jim Forest, explains how "it is prayer just to look attentively at an icon and let God speak to you." But there are

> "Art does not reproduce the visible, but makes visible that which is not easily seen."
>
> –KIMON NIKOLAIDES

many ways to adapt this, both as a craft and as a spiritual practice, as artist and author Lisa Sonora Beam explains: "I happened to be reading novelist Haruki Murakami's engrossing memoir, *What I Talk About When I Talk About Running*. I've always admired people who like to run, and do marathons to challenge themselves. Reading Murakami's book got me thinking about what creative challenge would be my marathon equivalent.

"Initially, I started painting as a daily meditation and creative-practice experiment. I thought that this practice would be a kind of solo meditation retreat for myself, which I could do right in the heart of Los Angeles, where I was living at the time. After doing about a dozen paintings, the idea for the 1008 Paintings Project came into focus. I had found my marathon.

"When I was designing this creative challenge for myself, I wanted it to feel like a marathon, or like a long sitting meditation retreat. If you've ever done a long sitting retreat, you'll know it is just as arduous as running, but in a different way. What amount of paintings would constitute a marathon challenge? As I considered numbers, one hundred paintings didn't feel like enough of a marathon for me. When I considered doing one thousand paintings, that's when I felt the pang of excitement mixed with a touch of terror, a recipe that always lets me know I'm on the right track with a new idea. One thousand felt much more like a marathon to me. One thousand felt exactly like the reaction I get whenever I have considered doing a running marathon: no way can I do that. One thousand seemed even likely impossible, considering all the other responsibilities on my plate.

"When I got up to one thousand, it was a natural step to round up to 1,008, which is a sacred number in many spiritual and mystical traditions, especially in Buddhism. The number 1008 represents the infinite, and is said to contain the dimensions of the universe. I'm not a scholar on these things, but the number 1008 just felt right as I sat with it."

Lisa's paintings include a figure that looks like the silhouette of Buddha. Says Lisa, "So many people see these as little Buddha figures that my shorthand name for this project became simply, The Buddha Project. The Buddhist traditions teach about developing our

Buddha nature. This is done, in large part, through the practice of meditation. Meditation is an act of observing the mind and body without judgment, without interpretation. The meditator is literally sitting there, watching the mind. Breathing and coming back to the present moment. The act of meditation is one of those things that is simple and yet not easy. Especially after five minutes or thirty minutes, day after day for one, two, five, ten, thirty days.

"For me, these figures represent the person sitting with what is: the ups and downs of life, the myriad human conditions that affect us all, directly or indirectly at one time or another. They also represent the Buddha nature of the meditator. Whether a person meditates or not, we are all sitting with so much going on inside of us. Not literally sitting in meditation, but going about life with all of these thoughts and feelings and problems and challenges and joys and sorrows that no one else can see."

Whether you choose to craft a single icon, or 1,008, there will be mysteries to discover along the way. As Henri Nouwen wrote, "Icons are painted to lead us close to the heart of God."

Inner Inquiries for Journaling and Reflection

﹡ On what image—or on whose image—do I feel most called to contemplate right now in my life? Is it a form of some kind, or a face?

﹡ What do I notice when I gaze at that image? How does my awareness, appreciation, or understanding of it evolve or deepen?

Crafting a Spiritual Practice

"Connect your reason for crafting or creating to a higher purpose that draws you toward it. We have to have a good reason to do what we're doing, compelled by desire, rather than a sense of 'I should be doing this because it's good for me.'

"Create a container that supports your creative practice. By container, I mean structure. Structure is a specific time, place, duration, method of practice. It can take some amount of experimentation to find the time structure and method that truly feels supportive of your creativity. The reason we need a container, is that when we create, all sorts of discomforts tend to arise that cause us to immediately or gradually veer off course, away from the intention we originally set, away from our higher purpose.

"Read memoirs written by artists who also have some kind of spiritual or creative practice that they are wrestling with. Natalie Goldberg's memoir, *Long Quiet Highway*, is one I keep coming back to. Also, Pema Chodron's book, *When Things Fall Apart*, is something I've recommended to artists for years. You can read that book and substitute the word 'meditation' with whatever form your craft takes—writing, painting, sculpting, photography..."

—LISA SONORA BEAM

MESSAGES IN BOTTLES

The first piece of art I ever sold was an assemblage I made from a wooden box, holding a row of small glass bottles that were all filled with a curiosity, *a la* the artist Joseph Cornell (whose work I have always loved). Five cork-topped containers against a mirrored background each contained a mysterious element: a scroll with ancient writing, wrapped in a silver cord; bits of dried flora supporting a clay doll's face; a black-and-white image of a nineteenth-century couple kissing, surrounded by parrot-green feathers; a severed baby crab's claw, resting in white sand; a burgundy-stained cork nestled in dried red-rose petals.

Though I can't remember now the personal significance then of each image, when looking at a photograph of this piece now, I discover that they each still evoke a mood, a sense of awe, a wondering. Filling bottles with the ingredients of

> "This oceanic feeling of wonder is the common source of religious mysticism, of pure science and art for art's sake."
>
> –ARTHUR KOESTLER

life, whether as part of an assemblage or as a stand-alone reflection, can take one on some interesting journeys.

There is a romanticism connected to a bottle with a message in it—haven't we all dreamed of finding one washed up on a beach (or throwing one out to sea ourselves)? Songs, novels, and movies have all focused on the intrigue of sending out a personal message held in glass. But, when created as a spiritual craft, our "messages" can take on deeper meanings—you might want to explore something that you're aware of "bottling up," or something that you want to "let out of the bottle." Think of it as sending out your own personal SOS—Soul Offering to Spirit.

Inner Inquiries for Journaling and Reflection

* Are there any messages that I long to express in my life—a message of hope, or a message that I need help?

* If I were to convey this message visually, what would it look like? What elements would best represent it?

* Do I want to keep my message to myself, or share it? With whom would I want to—and with whom would it be safe to—share it?

DIY: Crafting a Message in a Bottle

There is an endless array of glass containers available for use in this craft—from tiny, inch-high bottles with a *teeny*-tiny cork top intended for jewelry-making, to small three- to five-inch bottles made for spices, to yet larger sizes still. The size you choose will define the materials that you are able to include inside.

Looking at Patterns

"I have developed various 'crafty' spiritual practices; I have made beading a spiritual practice, and recently I've begun using shadow boxes for this purpose. I love to take pictures, so I use one of my photos (usually flowers, trees, sunrises or sunsets, or other natural wonders) as the backdrop and will add sticks that I decorate with glitter or wrap with colored thread, crystals, shells, and beaded feathers. As I create each of these shadow boxes I am in prayer for the person or people I create them for. I might also add a quote that is relevant to the occasion or person.

"This year I created boxes to commemorate the New Year as gifts for my workmates. I find that creating these boxes has become a way to allow the receiver to know that I 'see' them and can give a piece of myself to them through the practice of prayer on their behalf as I make them."

–FRANNE KETOFSKY EHRLICH DEMETRICIAN

"It is by using and developing our creative soul gifts that we can be fully empowered to jointly create a more wholesome world… These soul gifts are the means through which we manifest our individual sparks of divine light."

–JUDITH CORNELL

CRAFTING FOR COMMUNITY

Chapter 6:

CRAFTING FOR COMMUNITY

"The most basic lesson that all art teaches us is to stop, look, and listen to
life on this planet, including our own lives, as a vastly richer, deeper, more
mysterious business than most of the time it ever occurs to us to suspect
as we bumble along from day to day on automatic pilot. In a world that
for the most part steers clear of the whole idea of holiness, art is one of
the few places left where we can speak to each other of holy things."
–FREDERICK BUECHNER

THOUGH ALL OF OUR CREATIONS BECOME COMMUNAL THE
moment another pair of eyes stops to look at them, making art in community—or for
a community—is a far more rare experience. Too often we think of the stereotypical
depiction of the artist as a solitary soul, often emotionally tortured (or at least driven),
someone who doesn't fit in, someone with a tendency toward self-destruction.

Communal art- and craft-making turns that stereotype on its head, particularly when
done as a spiritual practice. There, in community, each creator finds a commonality of
purpose and language...a sense of being part of the whole, but with an individual perspective to share. More than that, it can birth something of importance to the community—

a new way of looking at things and/or of looking at each other. As Matthew Fox writes, "To speak of creativity is to speak of profound intimacy. It is also to speak of our connecting to the Divine in us and of our bringing the Divine back to the community."

> "Creativity belongs to the artist in each of us. To create means to relate. The root meaning of the word art is to fit together and we all do this every day. Not all of us are painters but we are all artists. Each time we fit things together we are creating—whether it is to make a loaf of bread, a child, a day."
>
> —CORITA KENT

All of the crafts in this chapter can be adapted for use by an individual, but they are far more powerful when their creation and use is in the company of others. (And the "Inner Inquiries for Journaling and Reflection" in this chapter are geared to communal answers.) You may find, as you explore these community exercises that, as artist Corita Kent put it, "Doing and making are acts of hope, and as that hope grows, we stop feeling overwhelmed by the troubles of the world. We remember that we—as individuals and groups—can do something about those troubles."

TALKING STICKS

The use of a "talking stick" comes from the Native American tradition; it is a tool used when gathered as a group that honors the contribution of each group member. The talking stick is passed to each person as that person speaks, and only the person who is holding the stick is allowed to speak at that time. The intention behind the talking stick is to let everyone's voice be heard; while one is not required to agree with what's being said, one is required to be silent during the speaking of it. Talking sticks (sometimes other objects are used for this purpose, such as a hand-held stone) will vary according to the material being used; it can be a powerful experience to make your own talking stick or to create one in community for use by that community.

In the Native American tribal traditions, there are qualities associated with the different woods that the stick may be made of; for example, cedar represents cleansing, maple represents gentleness, and elm represents wisdom. Sticks from fruit trees represent abundance; sticks from evergreen trees represent continued growth. Choosing a wood that will reinforce the group's intention as a collective is an important way to start the process and spiritual practice—for already an important dialogue has begun.

> "Creativity is so much more than art making. It is a tool for navigating through everyday experiences to find the sacred in each God-given moment."
>
> –KARLA M. KINCANNON

Colors also have particular associations: for instance, white can represent spirit; purple, healing; red, life; and blue, wisdom. And any animal hair or hide that is used with a talking stick is believed to bring the abilities—the "medicine"—of those particular animals with it: Snakeskin wrapped around the talking stick will heal and transmute any illness of body, mind, or soul; and rabbit fur is especially helpful for talking-stick use, as it brings the ability to listen with big ears!

Inner Inquiries for Journaling and Reflection

* What is the deepest intention for this group? What do we hope to manifest by coming together in community?

* Given our intention, what materials would best support our deepest reasons for gathering together? What colors? What animal "medicine"?

* How can we ensure that everyone plays a part in the creation of the talking stick?

* What do I personally feel when handling the talking stick that everyone has helped to create?

DIY: Crafting a Talking Stick

The elements to use on the talking stick can be found on a nature walk on land where it is acceptable to take the natural items found. Surveying the ground or beach on which you walk, dead wood from fallen trees, driftwood, feathers, shells, and seedpods can all be collected as elements for your stick.

When assembling the stick, clean it if necessary, peel away any bark, and sand it until smooth, letting everyone in the group take a turn. Special words, quotations, or verses can be carved, burned, or written on the wood.

When decorating, let each person offer an intention for the elements he or she includes. Tie these onto the stick or use craft glue to affix items that can't be tied. There should be an unadorned space left at the top of the talking stick to allow it to be comfortably held.

A variation of this activity is the making of a peace pole, a visual representation of the community to walk in peace with others. As with the talking stick, each person can add his or her intention to the talking stick or peace pole and choose colors and elements that will best fulfill that intention.

Flashes of Inspiration

"As the situations in the Middle East started to spiral downward throughout the first decade of the twenty-first century, I was spiritually motivated to 'pray the news'—especially when forty U.S. soldiers were killed within one month in 2009. It became my daily mission to go to church and pray for peace. The beautiful votive lights at church felt more conducive to carrying my prayers than ordinary overhead electric lights—light is clear, translucent, and provides us with a better lens to see how the world works. Just as God is invisible (yet visible through other people), praying in the flickering candlelight feels like a more powerful environment in which to convey the invisible (yet visible through people like me) support that we have for our troops. Continuing this practice at home by creating a prayer space using the light of specially dedicated candles to address the darkness in the world makes good prayer sense to me!"

—MONIQUE FELIX

PRAYER-RIBBON WEAVING

Baskets of fabric strips, roughly thirteen inches long and just over an inch wide, are placed near a large metal grid. Community members are invited to take a fabric strip, to write a prayer on it using permanent markers that are placed near the baskets, and then to weave it into the metal frame where it joins the strips—the prayers—of others.

I first experienced the power of creating a communal prayer-ribbon weaving at a conference held for an international membership organization. After the prayer-ribbon weaving was created and beheld, we were invited to take a turn at dismantling it—to take home a prayer ribbon, that we might keep this memory and prayer alive. I remember closing my eyes and letting myself be guided to the one

> "Day after day your devotion to creativity will enable you to merge with your Creative Self. Your destiny will unfold from within. Your life will become the unique work of art it was meant to be."
>
> —LUCIA CAPACCHIONE

that would have the needed message for me. Indeed, the strip I chose had a word I reflect on often—"grace"—and this ribbon is beside me as I type this, draped on my bulletin board.

This craft can support any number of group purposes; its power lies in the tactile and visual pleasures of the fabric used, in the heartfelt messages that are written upon them in different "voices" and different handwriting, in the reaffirmation of being a part of something larger than ourselves when viewing the weaving as a whole. Just as ribbons often mark the pages of our beloved spiritual books, a prayer-ribbon weaving marks the moment in time when we gathered with others, known and unknown, and lifted our hearts together in prayer.

Inner Inquiries for Journaling and Reflection

*   Is there any particular cause or concern for which we will do a prayer-ribbon weaving? (For instance, one could be done for a general prayer—such as peace on earth—or for a specific concern, such as a country affected by a natural disaster.)

*   How will we ask people to contribute to the prayer-ribbon weaving?

*   What will be the ritual behind it—will we ask people to take a prayer ribbon home with them, or keep the frame up so that more and more ribbons can be added?

Looking at Patterns

"Weaving is my meditation, my salvation from depression, and my hope for the future of community.

"When I started my weaving business, I knew that there was something different about this venture. I had started and run other businesses with varying levels of success, but this one had spirit. There was a tiny voice in the back of my head telling me that this business would be the one that changed my life and the lives of others in my community.

"At the time I was recovering from the failure of a previous business, living in San Francisco, and working for minimum wage. I knew I didn't belong in the city so I set out to start a business that I could easily move to the country. I also wanted to do something that would let me be creative every day and form the foundation of the sacred crafts collective that I had dreamt of for over a decade.

"At some point in the process of weaving small items to raise money for my production equipment, I realized that I wasn't depressed any more. Exercising my creative potential seemed to be relieving my depression. I'm not a doctor and I can't tell people that creativity will cure their depression, but I can say that it made mine manageable.

"When I realized this, I set a goal for myself: exercise my creativity every single day. I believe that every time we engage in the act of creation we are connecting with the divine creator and strengthening the divinity in ourselves.

"Once the business was off the ground and others could see a tangible manifestation of my vision, they started appearing and talking about a spiritual community that used craftwork to connect to the sacred. We committed to each other and began the steps toward living together and creating a new community.

"Now that we have had some time together, I can report that, as a spiritual practice, creating in a group is not much different than creating on my own. My personal moments of connection with the divine still mostly happen during the time that I spend alone with the threads, letting my muse guide me in my work.

"The differences mostly lie in the mundane day-to-day aspects. When I crafted alone, my work and my goals were limited to my own imagination. Now, there is a community that cares, not just what I do, but why I do it.

"We help each other with every task from evaluating potential designs to critiquing photography, reviewing business decisions, and much, much more. They help shake me out of my own thought process and become a better artist than I could have ever been on my own, and to always remember our community goals in my process.

"We do have one community practice that enhances my personal spiritual work. In this group, we make it a point to acknowledge the sacred in each other.

Everyone has a different way of connecting with the divine and these differences serve as constant reminders that nobody's way is better than anyone else's.

"As part of our practice, we set aside time to share our spiritual experiences with each other and celebrate the diversity of spirit. Nobody's reality is judged by the others, but simply shared. This seemingly simple practice does more than anything else to take our individual threads and weave them into a community experience.

"In woven cloth, every thread in the warp touches every thread in the weft. If a thread is removed, the quality of the cloth is changed and weakened. In a close community, every person's life touches every other. They cannot be separated without changing and weakening the group. We hold it as a constant goal to develop our close community and then teach others how to do this for themselves.

"Many people have asked about contacting us, coming to visit, or joining the group. For now our community is cloistered while we do the work of developing a structure that will allow us to share and grow when the time comes. While we develop our community, we are always doing the sacred craftwork and going out on weekends to bring our vision into the world for others to see."

–BLOSSOM MERZ, "THE WEAVING MONK"
(ORIGINALLY PUBLISHED ON CRAFTINGTHESACRED.COM. USED WITH PERMISSION.)

COLLAGE MANDALAS

Anyone who's ever looked through a kaleidoscope and seen the intricate galaxies of color and shape will understand instinctively the power of making mandalas. Indeed, working with mandalas has become so popular that there are a number of mandala "coloring books" that can be ordered for children and adults alike, as well as mandala books and kits.

A mandala—a Sanskrit word meaning circle, with roots meaning "essence" and "container"—is an ancient symbol of wholeness that has been created and contemplated by Hindus and Buddhists for thousands of years. And modern-day mystics are finding mandalas helpful for spiritual understanding, as well; psychologist Carl Jung felt that "the mandala is the path to the center, to individuation...the exponent of all paths."

Creating mandalas can be done in a variety of ways, including using white pencils to draw them on black paper, colored pencils or pastels to draw them on white paper, or even using colored sand to experience the practice undertaken by Tibetan Buddhists and Navajo Indians—who, as a meditation on impermanence, create intricate sand mandalas only to destroy them.

> "Making art then becomes a communicating bridge so that the conscious and unconscious can inform and inspire each other. In art, our being and experience, seen and felt, find color, movement, relationship, and form."
>
> —CAROL A. SAGAR

When I was attending graduate school, I experienced the power of making collage mandalas as part of a collective during a group exercise. Each of my classmates was given a wedge-shaped piece of paper, a "piece of the pie," on which they were invited to collage their experience of the Divine. When everyone had finished their own pieces, all of the pieces were assembled together to create the whole—a round globe of colors and imagery with a range of beauty and diversity that was breathtaking. As I look now at the paper wedge that was my contribution to the mandala, I see a flock of floating water lilies, a spiderweb made crystalline with dewdrops on the filaments, an arched doorway with a patch of light on the other side, a wide-eyed infant in a pink hooded sweater oblivious to (or perhaps amused by) the mud on her face. It tells me something still about my conceptions of the Divine—and when placed in the collective "pie," the completed mandala was awesome in its variety of different sacred images.

Another way to use mandalas in community is by coloring individual mandalas while gathered together. At my church, we hold Sacred Sisters gatherings every other month during which someone who has volunteered gives a presentation. On the Sunday afternoon that two women had chosen to talk about mandalas, a beautiful array of black-and-white mandala patterns was fanned out on the tables, along with colored pencils and pastels. When exploring mandalas, you may find yourself feeling as one woman did—who listened as politely as she could, then asked, "When do we get to color them?"

Inner Inquiries for Journaling and Reflection

✳ What is the intention behind our mandala making? What do we hope this process will foster?

✳ Do we want to make a collective mandala, or work on individual mandalas in community?

✳ How will we create our mandalas—what format (such as collage) or materials (such as colored pencils) will best reflect our intention for creating the mandala(s)?

Guides for the Path

If you'd like to learn more about creating mandalas as a spiritual practice, two excellent places to start are Judith Cornell's book, *Mandala: Luminous Symbols for Healing* (Quest Books, 1994), and *Creating Mandalas: For Insight, Healing, and Self-Expression* by Susanne F. Fincher (Shambala, 1991). There is also a lovely series of themed mandala books published by Duncan Baird; look for *Healing Mandalas* by Lisa Tenzin-Dolma (Duncan Baird, 2008).

GROUP PRAYER BEADS

When I turned forty, I invited twenty women in my life to celebrate that "coming of age" with me, and I asked each one of them to bring a bead to string on a strand that I would use as my personal prayer beads. The result was so deeply touching, and diverse, that it moves me still—no two beads are alike, unless they were bought and given as a pair (and one matching pair of hematite beads was, to remind me of balance); and the spectrum of choices ranged from a small megaphone-shaped brass bead to remind me "to always make your voice heard" to a miniature glass peppermint, to remind me of the sweetness of life.

The delight and significance of prayer beads is no less concentrated when making group prayer beads, as I discovered the first time I helped a community to create them during a weekend women's retreat I facilitated for a large Bay Area church. As part of the retreat, each woman made her own strand of prayer beads, but then I asked

> "To me art is one of the great resources of my life. I feel that it enriches the spiritual life and makes me more sane and sympathetic, more observant and understanding."
>
> —ABBY ALDRICH ROCKEFELLER

them to create a communal strand, one that every woman contributed to and prayed over, as a special token of the community each woman was a part of. It was my hope that should a woman be facing a particular challenge in her life, she could borrow the communal prayer strand and be reminded that she was part of a community and had the prayers of those others around her and supporting her.

When doing this craft, it's helpful to lay the groundwork for how the group prayer beads will be used once completed—and to specify the intention for which the beads are being made. You could even use the chapters of this book to help define this: Are they being made to calm, comfort or to help with clarity or contemplation? Once the intention is agreed upon and stated, each person will have a guide for what and why each bead is chosen. Holding a circle during which the meaning behind each bead is explained—and later having those descriptions typed up to accompany the group prayer beads—is a powerful way to let each heart be heard.

Inner Inquiries for Journaling and Reflection

* What do I receive from this group I'm in?

* What do I give to this group?

* How can this group better minister to each member?

* How can this group better minister to those outside of it?

Looking at Patterns

"I always concentrate on people who will receive the piece I'm crafting, if I'm doing so for other people. But when my mother died, we decided to wait two months to have her memorial, so everyone would be around. I had cared for Mom as she lived into the end of her life with Alzheimer's...in the last two years of her life, I had fed her meals every day; and we sang show tunes constantly. She was delightful and I missed her dreadfully; Mom had always been a great friend. I decided to put my grief to work in that waiting period and designed and made necklaces with turquoise in them for all of the women my mother Betty had loved. (I made pins with turquoise beads for the men in her life.) In those two months, I probably made forty necklaces and twenty-five pins. It was so soothing. Betty loved turquoise; everyone knew that. So everyone had fabulous Betty necklaces or pins for her memorial. It was a wonderful thing for me—a wonderful way to tie us together. (*And* I think most of the necklaces held together!) It was a way for me to acknowledge Betty's connections and my grief. At the end of the memorial, which was also a work of love for her, I was done with much of my heavy mourning."

–ANN KEELER EVANS

Prayer Arrows

"It is rare for Native Americans to call themselves 'artists,'" Frank Menusan relates. "That is because in our culture, art is a democratic process—everyone creates beauty and harmony in their life." I feel extremely fortunate to be having this conversation with Frank, as he is telling me about prayer arrows—a Native American handcraft used specifically for prayer—which have not often been written about.

Frank, of Muskogee (Creek) heritage, has made it his life mission to be a bridge between cultures—and he does this in the unlikely environment of New York City. A retired special-education teacher with a master's degree from New York University, Frank is also an accomplished musician, flute maker, artist, writer, storyteller, and lecturer.

Frank tells me how the prayer arrows are begun, with a cane reed that is hollowed out then wrapped with yarn or silk thread. With every revolution of the thread, a prayer is said; as Frank says, by the time you reach the point of the prayer arrow, "you feel like you have really prayed your way to it!"

Once the prayer arrow has been wrapped, prayers are breathed into it, and tobacco—considered a sacred, healing plant—is placed within the reed's core. After plugging the ends with beeswax, the prayer arrow is capped with feathers. According to Frank, different types of feathers represent different intentions for the prayer arrow; an owl feather represents protection, a crane feather represents peace, a hawk feather represents healing, and an eagle feather represents Divine messages. Sometimes the prayer arrows include a stone arrowhead, made from chipping away the parts of the stone that are unnecessary or unusable—much like parts of us are chipped away as we grow and evolve.

Indeed, Frank says, every aspect of a prayer arrow and other forms of Native American handcrafts "are encoded with the wisdom and stories of the ancestors; just as each feather represents a different prayer intention, so do the colors of the yarn or thread being used. Yellow can represent infancy, the direction east, or the element of fire; red can represent adolescence, the direction south, the element of water or blood; black can represent adulthood, the direction west, or the element of earth; and white, eldership, the direction north, or the element of air or spirit." Thus an entire story can be read in the very elements of the prayer arrow—with a thoughtful glance at the elements used, one can discern the prayer arrow's meaning and message.

Unlike some of the other crafts in this chapter, prayer arrows aren't usually made in community (although they can be), but rather are made for the benefit of a community. The prayer arrows are usually put in a bundle that can be held individually, or in a tribal bundle in trust for the entire community. They are left at sacred places of pilgrimage, and can be simple or ornate. They are also used as offerings, and given to others as protection or blessings.

> "Art making allows us to give in to the mystery, through which we renew our connection to feelings of both wonder and well-being."
>
> −CATHY A. MALCHIODI

Frank remembers the time when, as a teacher, he made prayer arrows for a student who was notorious for rebellious and difficult behavior in the classroom. Throughout that year, Frank made prayer arrows for the boy and kept them hidden in a locked location, in addition to keeping pinches of tobacco—considered a sacred plant—in the windowsills. Through this, Frank was holding the intention to make the space sacred—and the boy's behavior was never a problem again. "People can't see sacred," Frank relates, "but they sure can feel it. This is the power behind these objects—they keep the intention, the energy activated. By doing these things, we're making an offering."

No matter how they're used or where they're placed, the primary power of prayer arrows lies in their gift of refocusing all the concerns in one's life—because you are saying a prayer with every wrap of the reed. In that sense, Frank likens them to a Tibetan prayer wheel, which sends prayers into the air with every turn of the wheel. "Every time you wrap that arrow, you can pray 'Thank you, Creator, for my health; thank you, Creator, for this day'…keep continuing until you're saying thank you for the sun, the planets, the cosmos—for the blessings to the edges of infinity!"

Inner Inquiries for Journaling and Reflection

* ❋ For what—or for whom—am I called to pray at this time in my life?

* ❋ What is the intention behind my prayer—healing, protection, wisdom? What elements and colors would best support the intention of my prayer?

* ❋ In what areas am I being "chipped away"? How might I be becoming more useful because of this spiritual pruning?

"The purpose of the craft is not so much to make beautiful things as it is to become beautiful inside while you are making those things. The finest examples of craftsmanship that come down to us through the ages exalt the human spirit. They belong to us all. They show what we are capable of and what we deserve."

—SUSAN GORDON LYDON

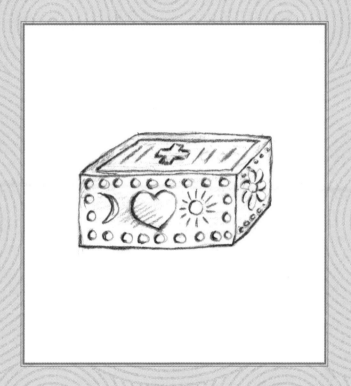

CRAFTING FOR CONNECTION
WITH OTHERS

Chapter 7:

CRAFTING FOR CONNECTION WITH OTHERS

"Our gifts are not from God to us, but from God through us to the world...
'your part' is to honor and develop the artist within you."
–JANICE ELSHEIMER

THE CONCEPT OF CRAFTING FOR CONNECTION WITH OTHERS differs somewhat from crafting for community; in the practices we have just explored, all of them become a vehicle not only for creating but for creating community—knitting together lives as one works with others on a creative project. In this chapter we are looking for practices to help us create a connection *to* others—whether that "other" is simply another, or many others.

Crafting for connection with others can even become a sacrament, a holy honoring. As art teacher and author Adriana Diaz writes, "Love is a sacrament. Beauty is a sacrament. Peace is a sacrament. Creativity is a sacrament. These things course through us just as surely as our blood. These are our sacred bonds with the divine and with each other: they are sacraments administered by the divine through the human."

Indeed, when one reflects on the history of handcrafts, they were—and still are—often made as gifts for another. What parent doesn't cherish the first wobbly popsicle-stick box or "eye of God" weaving made proudly by their child? There is something innately special about something that was made by someone, for someone, especially when that someone is *you*.

In this chapter you'll read about five different crafts that make particularly good gifts for another,

"In the eyes of the Creator, each person's gift is equally important, even though one person's might be to rule a nation while another's is to shape simple pots from clay, and still another's might be to raise a family. Bringing forth our gift is absolutely essential for making the Universe whole and complete."

—HAL ZINA BENNETT
AND SUSAN J. SPARROW

that serve well for making a connection to another that will be reinforced whenever that item is used. For it is in the giving that we truly extend our hands…and our hearts.

THINKING-OF-YOU CANDLES

The image of a flame evokes immediate memories: of a campfire, a Christmas fire, a deliciously scented candle. And often those memories have a spiritual flavor, as candles used in most religious rituals reinforce an understanding that we are sparks of the Divine. Our very life force is often compared to

> "What happens in meditation is what happens in our acts of creativity: We become united with the Divine Spirit, which is the Spirit of Creation and Creativity."
>
> −MATTHEW FOX

a flame. And when exploring this subject of creativity and spirituality in our interview, artist Mary Anne Radmacher (see "Tabletop Altars" in the next chapter) compared *it* to a flame—believing that, just as the colors of a flame cannot be separated one from the other, neither can creativity and spirituality; they are conjoined within the same spark.

The power of candle making as a spiritual practice lies less in the process than it does in the practice, for making a candle can be as simple as melting down wax and adding any desired colors, fragrance, glitter, and stones or charms. But as noted above, the symbol of a candle is powerful, and its effects are magnified when personalized by you.

But just how to use candles, and candle making, as a spiritual practice? As Marie-Jeanne Abadie writes in *The Everything Candlemaking Book*, "There are many ways you can use your candles as a sacred art. For example, you can create a sacred space in your home to go to whenever the world is too much with you—to refresh your spiritual energies for the task ahead, to rest, to meditate, to reflect, to be silent and alone. Your handmade candles can be the perfect accompaniment…to put you in touch with your most peaceful center. By surrounding yourself with candlelight from candles of your own making, you connect with your inner self in a deep and significant way."

Whether you're making candles to support your own spiritual intentions or to give them as gifts, the association of light—our own and others' inner light—makes the craft of candle making especially meaningful.

Inner Inquiries for Journaling and Reflection

✳ Whose light shines brightly in my life?

✳ Whose light seems a little dim—who could use a "pick-me-up"?

✳ What is the quality of my own light these days?

DIY: Crafting a Thinking-of-You Candle

The popularity of candle making makes it easier than ever to craft your own candles, as you usually can find candle-making materials in hobby and craft stores. An easy way to make your own candle is to buy strips of colored beeswax to cut into your preferred size and then roll into a tube, making your candle. You can even add essential oils (see "Sacred Bath Salts" in Chapter One for the properties of some popular essential oils) or healing crystals or charms into the inner layers of the beeswax if you desire.

A variation on this theme would be to decorate plain votive candleholders with hand-made paper, ribbons, beads, and charms; whichever format you choose, you are bound to "light up" someone's face!

Flashes of Inspiration

"I returned to handcrafting by making scented candles. I give these candles to my friends and loved ones. My candle craft is extremely simple and frugal. For a few pennies, I can give the priceless gift of love!

"I use recycled wax and re-melt it down into new candles. I use recycled clear glass containers and pour the mixed wax into them, first placing a wick (or two) in the center of the glass jar or votive. I mix the wax and add colors according to what intention the candle has. For example, if it is a healing candle, I make it green; a candle for love or friendship, red; or a candle for serenity, blue.

"My favorite essential oils are vanilla and amber, which I combine and call 'vamber.' I add this to the warming wax. My favorite craft store is Juniper Tree in Berkeley. This is where I buy my oils, wicks, and glitter. Just before the candle cools completely, I add glitter to the top layer. I gift these candles to family and friends with a note of intention (healing, love, etc.) and tell them that when the candle burns down, to bring it back and I will make a new candle. I call them my 'eternal flames.'"

–BRENDA KNIGHT

PRAYER PILLOWS

Just like our affirmation blankets, crafting a prayer pillow for ourselves or others is a loving thing to do and a delightful gift to receive—for, as with a quilt or blanket, a pillow connotes the idea of rest, of release, of renewal.

I first explored this idea when looking for a prayer pillow for my daughter when she was a toddler. Doing a search on Ebay.com (one of my favorite research tools!), I found and ordered one that would literally vocalize a prayer when pressed. When the pillow arrived—a large pink-and-purple square of fuzzy fabric, edged in white eyelet—the recorded voice sounded a little creepy, and the pillow has since been discarded, but I still find great promise in the craft of making a prayer pillow.

> "The artist is not a special kind of [wo]man, but every [wo]man is a special kind of artist."
>
> —MEISTER ECKHART

Perhaps it was the recorded voice that threw the intention off; as a prayer pillow's power lies in its being personal, a place to hold *your* (or your recipient's) personal prayers. This "holding" of prayer can be encouraged in a number of ways: through a favorite prayer embroidered or painted on the pillow, or by creating a pillow with a pocket for prayers to be slipped in.

However you choose to work with your prayer pillows, may they bring you comfort and spiritual rest. The words of the oft-recited children's prayer "Now I lay me down to sleep" (the same prayer that was recorded in my unfortunate Ebay pillow, by the way) may take on a whole new dimension when laying your head on a pillow that you've created and infused with prayer.

Inner Inquiries for Journaling and Reflection

✳ What are some of my favorite prayers? What prayers do I find especially comforting?

✳ What prayers do I say at the conclusion of a day? What prayer would be a restful one to hold in my heart as I "lay me down to sleep"?

MILAGROS BOXES

> "God created the arts in order that life might be held together by them, so that we should not separate ourselves from spiritual things."
>
> –ST. JOHN OF THE CROSS

I adored *milagros* even before I understood what they were; perhaps they appeal to me because of their smallness, since they are usually dollhouse-sized, flat metal representations of the shifting sands of all that can concern humanity in life— children and pets, hearts, eyes, lungs and breasts, livestock and houses and heads. Being a longtime collector of Mexican folk art, I first encountered *milagros*—the Spanish word for "miracles"—on a small wooden cross bought on one of my travels, covered on every square inch with every imaginable kind of these little metal shapes.

Milagros come out of Mexico and South America and are often seen in the handcrafts of those cultures; they are used to represent current prayer requests and are also used as symbols of thanksgiving, to denote answered prayers. As writer Helen Thompson notes, *milagros* are "symbolic of a covenant between a believer and a higher spirit."

I have used *milagros* often in my art and craft projects; and I have enjoyed using them as both an element of, and purpose for, boxes—boxes to hold prayers, boxes to hold dreams. I wrote this artist's statement years ago about a box I made for an auction that was covered in *milagro* hearts: "For this piece and its theme of hope, I wanted to celebrate the resiliency of our human hearts—their ability to recover strength and spirit and to generate new dreams. Personally I am nourished and inspired by the folk art of Mexico, so I used some elements often found in it—the *milagros*, bottle caps, and bright colors—to convey that sense of affirming life, no matter what we may be experiencing in the moment. The pictures of children inside the bottle caps represent our children—and the childlike part of ourselves—whose hopes for the future can change the world. By placing a mirror (an element I use often in my work) in the bottom of the 'hope chest,' everyone who looks at it becomes a part of the piece and, hopefully, is reminded of his or her own resilient heart!"

If you're not called to explore *milagros* by decorating a box with them, a variation of this practice can be crafting a beaded prayer strand, which incorporates *milagros* (see also "Intention Jewelry" in Chapter Five). When a friend of mine was going into the hospital to have surgery on her leg, I made her a beaded prayer strand with a little *milagro* of a leg on it. This was a symbol that she could hold or hang by her bed that represented both the prayer—for successful surgery (which that surgery was)—and an affirmation of that prayer being answered.

Inner Inquiries for Journaling and Reflection

＊ What is the deepest prayer of my heart right now? Is it about relationships? Health? Home? A pet?

＊ Which of my prayers have been answered? Have I expressed gratitude for that? What would be the best symbol I could use to give thanks?

DIY: Crafting a Milagros Box

Make a box—a *milagros* box—to celebrate the miracles in your life, or to use as a place in which you keep your written prayers. You can find hinged boxes in any craft store; paint or stain it in the colors that will best suit the purpose for the box. To make your box look like a reliquary, cover the top with crumpled aluminum foil that has then been flattened out and cut to size, then brush black or brown paint over it to "age" it. Add the *milagros* that are most meaningful to you using strong crafter's glue, and attach glass gems if desired.

Guides for the Path

For more on *milagros*, check out *Milagros: A Book of Miracles* by Helen Thompson (HarperSanFrancisco, 1998). You can also buy and learn about *milagros* on the website of Zanzibar Trading Company, zanzibartrading.com; they carry a wide range of *milagros* and have an extensive listing of what particular *milagros* symbolize (for instance, a *milagro* of a dog could mean a family pet, but a dog *milagro* could also symbolize loyalty or protection).

HOMEMADE BREAD MEDITATION

Though it is another craft that I personally profess no talent in, the culinary arts also lend themselves to spiritual practice, as anyone who ever read or saw the movie *Like Water for Chocolate* knows. As

> "Where the spirit does not work with the hand there is no art."
> –LEONARDO DA VINCI

Lynn M. Brodie put it, "When I cook I am part of the interconnecting past, present, and future of humanity. I have opened a window to my own inner soul and to the world around me. I am completely involved in the activities of life and paying close attention to all that surrounds me. By being fully present in the moment, I experience a peace, a connection, and a rootedness. Through this awareness I am connected with the ultimate forces of the universe within and without."

Regina Roman is a practicing spiritual director and travel guide, whose company leads pilgrimages around the world. Though she makes and sells beautiful strands of personal prayer beads, there is another craft—a simpler craft—that she turns to as spiritual practice: the making and giving of homemade bread. She describes how this developed: "Baking and cooking as a spiritual practice came so naturally that I did not know that was what I was doing. As a young child I would go with my grandmother to gather eggs from her chickens and pick strawberries from her garden to make her favorite strawberry cake. We talked about nature and the miracle of just one egg. She was a woman of great wisdom and her stories always captivated me. An egg was not just an egg; it was also a symbol for the human person.

177

"While holding an egg in her weathered hand, she would explain to me how our bodies, like the outer shell of an egg, are initially what the world sees. However, it is what is on the inside when mixed with the right ingredients that makes miracles happen. She would crack the egg and say, 'Soon this will be a delicious cake!' That was the miracle for her. Only later in life did I realize that the inside of the egg also represented my soul. When my inner being mixes with the right ingredients of love, joy, and purpose, miracles do happen and they are almost as delicious as a freshly baked cake.

"The spiritual practice of honoring all the ingredients in a recipe also led to the food becoming a sacrament in the sense that it was more than just something to eat; it was also a reminder of our deep connection to all of life. A few years ago, I wanted to offer a gift of hope to a friend, who was depressed and angry about life. I wanted to tangibly express the same peace and joy I had experienced—both from my grandmother and in the blackberry meadow I had played in as a child—in a gift. Of course, I baked a loaf of blackberry bread and wrote a poem about each of the ingredients. It became a primordial communion: 'Take this bread and eat, for it was made with loving devotion just for you. Let it become the love you need.'

"Baking bread is creating beauty to be consumed for joy, nourishment, and health. There is no transition from crafting to spiritual practice since my baking begins with the intentions of love, nourishment, and healing for the recipient. My attention throughout is on gratitude for all the amazing ingredients. When I reflect upon all the hands needed to bring me these ingredients, I am immersed within the web of life. The crafting is simply a prayer from beginning to end.

"Once the bread and poem is given as a gift, I know the prayer continues in ways I can only imagine. One recipient said it was like an entire liturgy, which made him feel in communion with all of nature. He felt connected and loved. This is when crafting as a spiritual practice flows from an inner awareness of self and God to an outer response through service."

Thus making bread—or any other similar baked good—can be so much more than feeding the stomach; it also serves as a way to feed someone's very soul. This practice lends itself so well to mindfulness meditation; both in the making of it and in the eating of it, we become connected to each other and to the earth itself.

Inner Inquiries for Journaling and Reflection

✳ Bread products can represent different things—for instance, rice cakes can represent health, as rice is believed to have healing powers; saltines can represent tears; sourdough bread can represent our roots. Ask yourself: Is there any particular food I could make that would represent an important association in my life (such as Regina's blackberry bread)?

✳ What family recipes do I cherish? What associations do I have with a treasured family dish—and why? How could those associations "feed" another?

✳ What food nourishes me in every way—physically, aesthetically, spiritually? What do I love about it? What memories does it bring back?

✳ Who in my life might need this sustenance now? For whom could I make it? How would I best explain to that person my reasons for making and giving it?

Crafting a Spiritual Practice

"My guidance? During crafting, step out of comfortable boundaries by first making the entire process a prayer (there is no right or wrong way to pray—it is more about an intention which will serve a higher good). Examples of prayer can include moments of gratitude for blessings, healing thoughts for the sick, or mindful breathing for peace in war-torn areas. Also, be open to the process and let it teach you something about yourself.

"Another way I approach my baking or cooking as a spiritual practice is to offer the entire process for the intentions of another person whose name I keep in mind. Or, I will write on a notecard my intention, such as 'gratitude,' and keep it in a visible place.

"Outer rituals can also help my inner awareness. They include taking a few deep breaths before I begin, lighting a candle as a touchstone to remind me of my intentions, and pausing periodically to say aloud my intentions, such as 'This bread is for Susan to welcome her home from the hospital. I bake it with healing and loving thoughts.'

"Crafting as a spiritual practice is like a pilgrimage; the journey is in the process, not the final destination. Each step is an opportunity to learn about who I am and the origin of the ingredients I use. Hydrogen was produced in the hot conditions of the birth of the universe, and when mixed with oxygen, forms the water I use in baking the bread. That thought of having an ingredient from the beginning of time is awesome. This deepens my connection with God."

—REGINA ROMAN

Guides for the Path

Two books Regina recommends for this practice are *The Spirituality of Bread* by Donna Sinclair ("This book reminds us that bread is a metaphor for spiritual formation as well as a conduit to bind us in communion with others") and *The Practice of the Presence of God* by Brother Lawrence ("This is a classic book, which for over three hundred years has shown countless readers how a humble monk encountered God among the pots and pans in everyday cooking").

Bread

Take this, precious one.
This bread was made for you, just for you.
With loving devotion, the elements of Mother Earth,
Together with the ingredients of the entire cosmos,
Have been mixed and kneaded just for you:
Water to quench your thirst when you are in the dry and lonely places,
Water flowing freely to bathe away your pain and sorrows,
Water to splash within when you just want to be childlike in your joy;
Grain to nourish you along the way,
Grain grown from the dark rich soils to inspire you,
Grain to re-call into you, after death is indeed rebirth;
Salt to preserve your one and only precious soul,
Salt harvested from the boundless sea to invite you back into the wild
    places,
Salt to enhance the essence of your entire being;
Yeast to bubble within, that you may grow into your fullness,
Yeast as a reminder of your perfect and absolute aliveness,
Yeast to rise into total abundance in your life.

183

Take this bread and eat.
Let it become the words too deep to capture in sounds.

Let the bread echo into the farthest reaches of your soul.
Let it be the LOVE you need.
Receive love and feast with wild abandonment,
Knowing your union with all,
For this bread was made for you, just for you.

©REGINA ROMAN, 2007

PRAYER STONES

Rocks and stones—such ancient, elemental ingredients of many of our cultural and spiritual practices. For they are accessible to us all; like shells on a beach, we all have been lit up by the joy of finding a rock or stone that spoke just to us—that had some kind of message, sometimes immediately discerned, sometimes mysterious—that prompted us to pick it up and put it in our pockets.

For many, a rock or stone is literally a touchstone—something that remains in our pocket or purse on a daily basis to remind us of a spiritual truth. For others, rocks or stones are displayed in a bowl or basket (many people collect heart-shaped stones), where they can be enjoyed by everyone who notices their singular beauty.

> "Creativity is a facet of the Divine intelligence of the universe. To create means to walk on holy ground, to engage with the Divine, and to experience it moving through me to manifestation."
>
> —PAT B. ALLEN

Used as a prayer stone, a simple rock becomes something we literally can hold on to—something that we can take into a doctor's office, finger while driving when at a stoplight, or place beneath our computer monitor to simply remind us to pray. This practice can also be a means of connection—you can give a prayer stone to another, which reminds that person not only to pray but also that he or she is not alone. (You can buy stones that have "I'm Praying for You" printed on them, but this craft calls out to be made personal by you: by writing your own sacred prayer on a stone, by painting your prayer on a stone, by adding texture to your stone with a glued-on rhinestone or crystal.)

However you use your prayer stone, and to whomever you give it, it is a simple reminder we have a Rock on which to stand…an ever-present strength to lean on.

Inner Inquiries for Journaling and Reflection

✳ What do I need to be reminded of during the day—what message brings me back to center?

✳ The late business coach Stephen Covey had an exercise in which he used stones: large rocks symbolize our non-negotiables, our deepest values, while small pebbles represent the myriad daily distractions that can divert our focus from what's truly important. Ask yourself: What are my "large rocks" in life? What are my "small pebbles"?

Prayer Rock Rhyme

I'm your little "prayer rock" and this is what I'll do;
Just put me on your pillow till the day is nearly through,
Then pull back the covers and climb into bed–
Whack! Your little "prayer rock" will hit you on the head.
This will remind you as the day is through,
It's time to say your prayers like you wanted to.
Then, when you are finished, just dump me on the floor
And I'll stay through the night to give you help once more.
When you get up the next morning, *clump* "I stubbed my toe!"
So you will remember your prayers before you get up and go.
Put me back on your pillow when your bed is all made.
Your clever little "prayer rock" will remain as your aid.
Because your Heavenly Father cares and loves you so,
He wants you to remember to talk to Him, you know.

–AUTHOR UNKNOWN

Looking at Patterns

"When my mother died in March of 2011, I spent several months in meditation and quiet contemplation. It was a time to stop all action in order to evaluate my life and become aware of how I was spending my time currency. This was an intense spiritual process of recognizing my entire life as a blessing. One of the major decisions that I made was to trust the Spirit and simply follow my joy and energy. That led me to make different choices about my time and career.

"I got my second level Reiki training in September of 2011. About the same time, I welcomed the artist within and returned to my gel-pen drawings on black paper, which I had stopped around 2003. I began to pray and ask the Spirit to work through me before I began to draw. At times it felt as if I was watching my hand paint on its own and knew what the next stroke should be. It was fascinating to go through the process of closing my eyes and seeing the first line on the paper and then see it develop into inspired artwork.

"In October, I began to paint ornaments to give as holiday gifts. In addition to saying a prayer before each session, I began to Reiki the ornaments. Meanwhile, I also painted a couple of snail shells that I had picked up from the shore of Hillsborough River. I put the pictures on Facebook and got many comments and messages, many asking me if they were for sale. My partner urged me to research the shells before I took them in large quantities. The idea was to make sure we were environmentally correct and that we would not be harming the ecosystem.

"In my research I found out that these shells were an invasive species of apple snails that were taking over the river and harming the ecosystem. So my removing them was actually an act of caretaking and good for the environment. That to me was a green light from the Spirit. I began to collect and paint the shells and post them on Facebook. Before I knew it, I began to get orders and a new business was born.

"I quickly learned that looking for shells was a process. For example, ruining one pair of shoes and having my jeans drenched with mud taught me to wear shorts and water shoes since most of the shells are found on the watery edges of the river under a canopy of trees where the water birds feel safe to eat their food. I begin with taking two trash bags to the river, one for shells and the other to collect garbage. Cleaning the river's edge is my way of caring for the earth and saying thanks for the shells. Before I start, I say a prayer of gratitude to the Spirit, the river, the birds, and the snails. Through it, I am completely aware of the gift that I am being given, grateful for the bounty of nature.

"The shells then are bathed in soapy water and bleach before being scrubbed clean. The rough edges and surface are sandpapered and the shell is ready for paint. Before beginning to paint, I say a prayer for each shell to become a source of beauty, joy, and healing energy to anyone that comes in contact with it. Then I infuse it with Reiki energy using the Reiki symbols. After I finish the several layers of paint, decoration, and varnishing, I hold the shell in my hand and ask for the meditation word that I then write inside the shell before I sign and date it.

"At this stage of my life, art is what excites me and connects me to my Source of creative energy. My hands, my heart, my intuition, and my spirit all line up to open a doorway for creativity to flow through me. The process of creation energizes me, and that energy transforms itself into my artwork.

"All creativity is a gift from the Spirit. Align yourself with your Higher Self and ask to be an instrument of Spirit and relax into your art."

—AFSANAH NOORI

"Handcrafting and decorating are not just frills—unnecessary additions to the curriculum of our lives—but fundamental to our awareness of basic forms, deep structures, and perennial patterns that could open up a new soul sensitivity in the realms of not only our personal lives, but also our cultural life and public policy."

—MARJORY ZOET BANKSON

CRAFTING FOR
CONNECTION WITH SPIRIT

Chapter 8:

CRAFTING FOR
CONNECTION WITH SPIRIT

"Art reaches toward God, where humanity touches divinity, and where the
intellectual fades to apprehending beauty. Art is important because it is a
pathway of mystical experience with God."
−DIANA BUTLER BASS

LAST BUT NOT LEAST, WE COME TO THE FINAL CHAPTER OF
the book that represents the first intention we make when crafting as a spiritual practice: to have our time of creation be a time to connect with Spirit. This is at the heart of
crafting as a spiritual practice—to use our hearts and hands and crafting materials as the
mediums through which we experience God. We come to the point where we feel, like
writer Ellen Morris Prewitt expressed it, that "I want something that does not involve
reading, study, endless discussion. I want a physical approach to God. A lady preacher
told me this physical type of prayer was called 'kinetic prayer.' When I researched what
kinetic prayer might be, I saw that she was right. I wanted an understanding that does not

come from parsing out an explanation for God, but arrives through a sensory, interactive experience of God."

This is an impulse that has occurred throughout time, throughout cultures, throughout spiritual traditions. As religious historian Karen Armstrong notes, it is in every tradition that "people turned to art when they tried to express or evoke a religious experience: to painting, music, architecture, dance, or poetry. They rarely attempted to define their apprehension of the divine in logical discourse or in the scientific language of hard fact. Like all art, theology is an attempt to express the inexpressible."

> "The arts draw us deeply into the parts of ourselves where our most urgent questions and desires lodge. These desiring questions have as their source and end, God."
>
> —WENDY M. WRIGHT

If you've read through this book, you've begun to see the possibilities for turning craft into a spiritual practice—or, if you've already been using your crafting as a form of spiritual practice, you've been introduced to new forms for it. Whatever your particular art form is, in the end we all arrive at the same place—the place where, as Janice Elsheimer put it, we realize that "Practicing your art is a form of worship, a way to use your talents to draw closer to God."

PRAYER OUTFITS

Ceremonial costumes have been integrated into religious rituals since the dawn of time. From the *kachina* masks of the Pueblo Indians to African *kente* cloth, adornments have been crafted for millennia for the express purpose of acknowledging the Divine.

> "The creative process, like a spiritual journey, is intuitive, nonlinear, and experiential. It points us toward our essential nature, which is a reflection of the boundless creativity of the universe."
>
> –JOHN DAIDO LOORI

While you might be influenced by historical and traditional forms of ceremonial costumes when crafting a special prayer outfit, your creativity can be channeled into any piece of clothing you choose—ranging from socks to stoles, T-shirts to tennis shoes. Indeed, I remember being both amused and intrigued when a colleague told me about the "magic shoes" that she made to symbolize how she was walking forth in her life, how she was expressing her soul's purpose. But as she said, "It doesn't have to be shoes; it could be robes, scarves, button covers. The point is to be bold and tell your creative truth: that's the prayer."

Embellished with beads, feathers, or sequins, adorned with a spiritual saying or not, *anything* can become a prayer outfit if that is the intention behind it. What's important is discovering what will be meaningful to you, what metaphor might be explored—such as the shoes that represent how the wearer is walking forth in life—in the wearing of it. And crafters of all types can appreciate the nineteenth-century words of Thomas Carlyle, that "A [wo]man cannot make a pair of shoes rightly unless [s]he do it in a devout manner."

Inner Inquiries for Journaling and Reflection

❋ How can I better mark my time alone with God? What special ritual can I include in my prayer or meditation time to distinguish it as holy?

❋ What are some of the associations I have for my spiritual path? Do I walk with God (if so, you may want to make prayer shoes)? Do I bow before the grandeur of God (if so, a head covering for prayer may be what you want to make)?

FINGER LABYRINTHS

As I enter my home office—my sanctuary, my studio—the first thing that I see as I enter is my textured rug, woven in colors of indigo and cream; and though smaller (approximately forty-eight inches in length), it is the exact pattern of the labyrinth at Chartres Cathedral. Labyrinths have played important roles in my life; I got married in San Francisco's Grace Cathedral (whose Rev. Dr. Lauren Artress is widely credited for resuscitating worldwide interest in the labyrinth as a spiritual tool), and my husband and I incorporated the cathedral's outside stone labyrinth into our celebration, walking it ourselves and asking our guests to join us.

People have been walking some form of labyrinth for four thousand years; the Christian use of labyrinths—such as that one at Chartres Cathedral—was for those who were not able to make a pilgrimage to the Holy Land, but who could experience a symbolic representation of that journey by walking a labyrinth. One of the most significant

> "Our soul emerges from this mysterious place inside us and out through our fingertips, ensouling the wood we carve, the gardens we cultivate, the children and animals and lovers we touch."
>
> –PHIL COUSINEAU

experiences I've had with a labyrinth involved creating one in community, with white flour on a grassy field; then walking it at midnight, passing the others who I knew but could not see, since the only illumination was moonlight.

When one is unable to walk an actual labyrinth, tracing the contours of one with one's finger can have the same meditative effect. For this practice, you can use a fabric labyrinth or craft a paper labyrinth using yarn to mark the bends and turns. You can also simply trace the pattern of a labyrinth with your finger (a number of patterns are available online); you might start a finger labyrinth notebook, in which you record the insights or awareness that result from the simple motions of your finger.

Whichever form of finger labyrinth you choose to create and use, mindfulness is key. Notice what thoughts come up, what feelings—use the time to be with God, and see where the journey leads you.

Inner Inquiries for Journaling and Reflection

✵ What journey of life am I in right now? Young adulthood? Parent-hood? Creating the final phase of my life?

✵ What are my fears about this journey; what do I need to support this journey?

✵ How do I feel about the nonlinear quality of a labyrinth—and of life? What do the twists and turns teach me?

Guides for the Path

To find a labyrinth in your area, log on to labyrinthlocator.com. It includes labyrinth locations around the world. Lauren Artress's book *Walking a Sacred Path: Rediscovering the Labyrinth as a Spiritual Practice* (Riverhead Books, 1995) will be a good reference, as will the resources of her organization's website, Veriditas.org.

PERSONAL HOLY BOOKS

As you might imagine—given that I am that woman who "lives with mottoes on the wall"!—I am a dedicated keeper of quotes, and though through the years the ways in which I've kept them have varied, it has always been in book form...my own private prayer book, if you will. Thus, when in 1999 I came across the book *Create Your Personal Sacred Text* by Bobbi L. Parrish, I was ecstatic: What better way to blend one's creativity with one's spirituality than to create one's personal book of spiritual wisdom?

As Parrish writes, "Creating a sacred text is...a unique process. There never has been, and there never will be, another human being exactly like you. Your thoughts, personality, ideas, and behaviors will go unduplicated for all of time. Consequently, no one has or ever will again have the understanding of and relationship with Spirit that you do. Your work will have a value unequal to anything else that will ever be done... Give the universe the gift of knowing who you are so we can all learn from your experience."

Through the years I have kept different kinds of personal holy books; some of them have been collections of prayers (I've also published two anthologies of prayer, *Prayers for Healing* and *Prayers for Hope and Comfort*, containing prayers from around the world and across traditions that you might find good references for your personal holy book), collections of spiritual quotations, a book of prayer concerns and of answered prayers, and a journal of collaged visual prayers. I've also worked with my

> "Everything which adequately expresses the inner need is beautiful."
>
> —WASSILY KANDINSKY

friend Janet Conner's book, *Writing Down Your Soul*, in which your personal holy book becomes a record of call and response—of your questions and of Spirit's answers.

As modern philosopher Deng Ming-Dao expressed it, remember, "All teachings are mere references. The true experience is living your own life." However you craft your personal holy book, it will be a book of illuminated pages in more ways than one.

Inner Inquiries for Journaling and Reflection

✳ How do I receive my inner guidance? Words, images, feelings? How can I capture that in a personal holy book?

✳ Do I have any prayer books or prayer journals that I use on a regular basis? How might I make these more personal to me?

Guides for the Path

The following resources may be helpful as you explore creating a personal holy book as a spiritual practice:

Faith Books & Spiritual Journaling: Expressions of Faith Through Art by Sharon Soneff (Quarry Books, 2006)

Scrapbooking Your Faith: Layouts That Celebrate Your Spiritual Beliefs by Courtney Walsh (Memory Makers Books, 2007)

Scrapbooking Your Spiritual Journey by Sandra L. Joseph (Reminders of Faith, 2003)

Looking at Patterns

"I use scrapbooking and art journals that I make to record different spiritual experiences. I make them for my whole family and we have a different one for each spiritual discipline or experience. We keep a decorated prayer journal to record or write out our prayers and how God answers them. We have a miracle journal to record various miracles that happen in our lives. I also will record various Bible verses and make vision board pages in my biblical art journal to correspond. That would look like using the verse 'Know ye not that your body is the temple ...' and then I would make a collage of different health related items, etc.; or 'I know the plans that I have for you' would translate into a collage of items we are hoping will manifest in our lives. I am an extremely visual person so turning Bible verses into visual works of art helps me to internalize their meanings so much more. I have also found that it's a great way to help my children understand Bible verses so much more. I give them magazines and a verse and let them make their own collages. It turns the Bible from some old book that's hard for them to understand into a real and living guidebook."

—KAY SAWYER ELLIOTT

TABLETOP ALTARS

Though the ways in which we can use the Internet to enhance our spiritual practices are still being discovered, it can be a useful tool for discovering new vehicles for exploration—and so it was in 2010, when I happened upon a Facebook post by artist and author Mary Anne Radmacher, focusing on her "altarariums"—or tabletop altars.

In the post she described using her altarariums for different intentions—and how blessed I felt when, after contacting her, she sent me an altararium, painted in shades of marine blue and teal with a large pink heart in the center. On the bottom of this tabletop altar is a heart-shaped stone, and a boldly marked word that is surrounded by glitter: "Intention." The key to every craft as a spiritual practice!

Mary Anne describes the journey she's been on since she was little: "I have been making things since I was a child. I believe the act of creating anything *is* a spiritual practice. Calling into being a new form from disparate or previously incompatible materials is a spiritual model. I didn't define creating as a spiritual practice when I was a child, but I intuitively turned to creating as a means of healing and solace. Then it became a way to sort my thoughts. Then…it became embedded into virtually everything I did."

Mary Anne's altarariums were a natural extension of her tendency to create altars everywhere she goes; she has one that stays in her writing room, she creates them in hotel rooms and any place she's staying of "whatever iconic images are calling to me at the moment." She continues, "My altar is not one thing…it's more of a practice than a thing. When I tell people I will pray for them, I write their names down and put them on my altar—in a clothespin glued on a rock—and I keep them there as long as they've indicated they need support."

She started creating her wooden tabletop altars out of a partnership with a woman who cuts the wood to specifications. But for those who are new to the practice of creating tabletop altars, Mary Anne recommends working with a simpler material first, such as making a small—say, five-by-seven-inch—triptych out of foam core or matte board. That, she says, will allow people to see if the practice of having a tabletop altar is something that they would like to incorporate into their lives. Even more basic "to create the methodology of a shrine," she advises those first exploring this to "Get a wooden bookstand and take a contemplative book that has meaning to you and open it up—to an image or paragraph that speaks to you."

How you construct your tabletop altar—whether it's wood or cardstock, whether it's an arrangement of small sacred items beneath your computer monitor or larger display on the top of a table—matters less than how you use it. What's important to keep in mind, as Edward Searl wrote, is that an altar is "a place of aspiration of and dedication to ideals. It's a place to bring and grow your soul."

> "So—out of nothing–all; existence from nonexistence. Thus the craftsman, from what in himself is metaphysical makes the tangible physical object."
>
> —P. L. TRAVERS

Inner Inquiries for Journaling and Reflection

✻ Remember Mary Anne's word, "Intention." Ask yourself: What do I want to craft an altar for? A specific project or concern? A seasonal altar? An altar that explores my understanding of the Sacred?

✻ Where will my altar best serve me? How can I interact in a meaningful way with my altar?

Guides for the Path

The following books may be helpful as you explore crafting a tabletop altar as a spiritual practice:

Altars: Bringing Sacred Shrines into Your Everyday Life by Denise Linn (Ballantine Wellspring, 1999)

Altars and Icons: Sacred Spaces in Everyday Life by Jean McMann (Chronicle Books, 1998)

A Place of Your Own by Edward Searl (Berkley Books, 1998)

Altars Made Easy: A Complete Guide to Creating Your Own Sacred Space by Peg Streep (HarperSanFrancisco, 1997)

Crafting a Spiritual Practice

"The guidance I would give to others who want to approach their craft as a spiritual practice is this: The desire that it should be so, makes it so. Brother Lawrence, in *The Practice of the Presence of God,* indicated that every act, when rendered to God, becomes a prayer. It is so with creating. When I am working on something specifically as a service or a compassionate outreach, I pray before I begin. I pray that my hands will find the way to communicate what the recipient needs to see and read. That prayer, conscious or unconscious, is part of almost everything I create. To inspire and motivate is built in to my compulsion to create. So, the prayer to inspire is as natural as the reach for a specific brush.

"I believe any spiritual practice becomes stilted when we try to delineate it or separate it out from our common experience. Epiphany. Awakening. These are not mystical encounters only available periodically. The ecstatic embrace of the Divine is always at the ready to be taken into our every experience. This is as true when I do laundry as it is when I lay out my paints and materials and begin to make Something Other from a Bunch of Somethings. We are Creators and are Creating a Life from the moment we awaken to the moment we fall ...into the grave."

–MARY ANNE RADMACHER

PRAYER POTS

The idea of a prayer pot is the same idea behind prayer boxes and prayer bowls—simply sanctifying a container as the holder of your heartfelt prayers. There is something about being able to hold your prayers, to cup your hands around your prayers, that reinforces the idea of openness and surrender—and a pot is a perfect shape to invite that.

Prayer pots or bowls have been used in a variety of cultures, ranging from Buddhist to Native American. And using an open container, such as a cup or chalice, dates back to the Greek and Roman heyday—inhabitants of both eras are said to have followed the practice of placing them

> "Art is not an end in itself. It introduces the soul into a higher spiritual order, which it expresses and in some sense explains."
>
> –THOMAS MERTON

on their altars. One of the most enchanting modern-day examples of a prayer bowl or pot is made by Huichol Indians, whose intricately patterned and colorful prayer pots are made with tiny seed beads.

The Huichols construct these beaded offerings under the influence of the hallucinogenic peyote; the use of this is always done reverently, as a means to communicate with Spirit.

I have a number of small Huichol pieces, including two tiny beaded bowls, and I even tried making a version of this type of prayer pot using a dried coconut-shell half as the bowl, melting sticks of beeswax, and placing a plethora of tiny seed beads in rainbow hues into the melted wax. I wrote about this for the "Soul Crafts" section of the magazine *Living Crafts*; what I did not say in the article is that after trying my hand at this—and discovering just how very tedious, time-consuming, and frustrating the process could be—I wanted to alter my consciousness too, but not for the reverent reasons the Huichols do!

But again, the product is not as important as the process of using it; and people who use a prayer bowl, box, or pot do so in different ways. Some write down their prayers and read through them later, to note how their prayers have been answered. Others like to use their container to hold their dreams for the future, writing down the desires of their hearts for safekeeping in sacred space. Still others like to write letters to their Higher Power, placing the letter in the pot to "let go" of their attachment to whatever concern they have written about. Explore these different methods, or create your own—the possibilities are as open as the mouth of the prayer pot itself.

Inner Inquiries for Journaling and Reflection

❊   What prayer concern am I too attached to? Where do I need to "let go and let God"?

❊   In what ways do I try to direct the affairs of my life, instead of trust? Do I need to practice more surrender, or do I need to "pray, then move my feet"?

❊   Do I have a way of acknowledging answered prayer in my life?

DIY: *Crafting a Prayer Pot*

As with many of the spiritual crafts we've looked at, an option for this practice is to find an existing pot and make it your own through adornments of your choosing—glitter glue; calligraphy in metallic permanent ink of the words of a special prayer; ribbon or yarn strands tied around the pot and strung with meaningful charms. But, if you yearn to create a pot yourself, you have several

> "Remember that as a creative person, the important thing is to create. Who sees what you make, where it goes, and what it does is a secondary consideration; the first is to exercise the talent God has given you."
>
> —FRANKY SCHAEFFER

choices: to use a potter's wheel to craft a pot and then fire it in a kiln; to do a "pinch pot" (consisting of coils of clay that are placed atop each other, then pinched together to hold the form) and then fire it in a kiln; or to buy a package of crafter's clay that will air-dry, most usually found in porcelain and terra cotta. For the latter, all you need is the clay and your imagination; your fingers, and fingerprints, will make it uniquely your own.

Conclusion

"Listen to your life. See it for the fathomless mystery that it is. In the
boredom and pain of it no less than in the excitement and gladness:
touch, taste, smell your way to the holy and hidden heart of it because in
the last analysis all moments are key moments, and life itself is grace."
—FREDERICK BUECHNER

IN MY HOME OFFICE THERE IS A SMALL POSTER HANGING ON
the wall that I face when I sit at my computer to write. It depicts a mixed-media piece by
the artist Sabrina Ward Harrison done in sepia tones, and on it is written this calligraphic
counsel: *Collect Your Life.*

All creations, everything we make from the basic
ingredients of life, are acts of intimacy—literally vehicles through which another can "into me,
see." Our lives themselves are the ultimate act of
creativity, and each of our lives is as unique as our

"You can be creative only if you
love life enough that you want to
enhance its beauty."
—OSHO

fingerprints. In this book I have offered bits and baubles collected from my life in the
hopes that they will spark something within each reader that inspires you, too, to sort
through the magnificent treasure box that is *your* life.

The dancer Martha Graham wrote a very compelling passage about why we need to honor "such stuff as dreams are made of"—and such stuff as our lives are made of. It's always because:

> There is a vitality, a life force, an energy, a quickening
> That is translated through you into action.
> And because there is only one you in all time,
> This expression is unique.
> And if you block it,
> It will never exist through any other medium…
> The world will not have it.
> It is not your business to determine how good it is,
> Nor how valuable,
> Nor how it compares with other expressions.
> It is your business to keep it yours clearly and directly,
> To keep the channel open.

What I've hoped to do in this book is to demonstrate that everything can be holy—that every moment we live can be holy—and all that we need to do to experience that state is to make the decision to do so. The golden thread running through every piece in this book is the word "intention"—that by making it our intention, we can truly "pray without ceasing." For every way that we can be "mindless" about something, there is a contrasting way to be mind*ful*—to approach everything in our lives as a spiritual practice.

Matthew Fox wrote, "There is a river of creativity running through all things, all relationships, all beings, all corners and centers of this universe. We are here to join it, to get wet, to jump in, to ride these rapids, wild and sacred as they be." So, too, there is a river of Spirit—all things, all relationships, all beings, all corners and centers of this universe are held in this holy Ground of Being. May you ride these rivers in love and trust as you explore these practices and create your own. As the poet Emily Dickinson once wrote, "We dwell in possibility." May this book be a potpourri of possibilities that helps you to daily dwell in the Divine.

> "Just as the religious person makes time for prayer during the day, the creative person makes time for expression... Art as spiritual exercise suggests that any person can find a way to make time for the creative act each day."
>
> —SHAUN MCNIFF

Resources

WEBSITES

Abbeyofthearts.com

Christine Valters Paintner's "monastery without walls," offering resources to nurture contemplative practice and creative expression.

Artheals.org

The online resource of the Arts & Healing Network, celebrating the connection between art and healing.

Crafting as a Spiritual Practice Group on Facebook

More interviews, ideas, and inspiration for crafting as a spiritual practice from Maggie Oman Shannon.

Craftingthesacred.com

Sacred creativity blog, coaching, and online workshops by Jo Crawford.

Crescendoh.com

Jenny Doh's blog, store, online classes, and other resources—because "art saves."

Explorefaith.org

A wonderful collection of articles on the spiritual life, including a "Meditate with Art" section.

Flickr.com/groups/manbroidery

A gathering place for the male crafter.

Janrichardson.com

The home of spiritual artist and writer Jan Richardson's various web offerings.

LivingCrafts.com

Ideas to "craft your whole life."

Makingisconnecting.com

A companion website for the same titled book by David Gauntlett that explores "the social meaning of creativity."

Spiritualityandpractice.com

The mother lode of spiritual websites featuring thousands of pages of resources gathered by Frederic and Mary Ann Brussat.

Spiritualityseries.com

Click on "The Spirituality of Art" to find a number of online practices.

Stampington.com

The main home of Stampington magazines (see below), and featuring online tutorials and craft store.

Magazines

Stampington & Company publishes a large collection of magazines that may provide inspiration as you pursue crafting as a spiritual practice; a few in particular to check out are *Art Doll Quarterly, Art Journaling, Artful Blogging, HandCrafted, Life Images, Somerset Life,* and *Somerset Studio.*

Books

Creative Exercises

The Artist Inside: A Spiritual Guide to Cultivating Your Creative Self by Tom Crockett (Broadway Books, 2000)

The Artist's Rule: Nurturing Your Creative Soul with Monastic Wisdom by Christine Valters Paintner (Sorin Books, 2011)

Creating Change: The Arts as Catalyst for Spiritual Transformation edited by Keri K. Wehlander (CopperHouse, 2008)

Creativity and Divine Surprise: Finding the Place of Your Resurrection by Karla M. Kincannon (Upper Room Books, 2005)

Making Things: A Book of Days for the Creative Spirit by Janet Carija Brandt (Martingale & Co., 2005)

Spirit Taking Form: Making a Spiritual Practice of Making Art by Nancy Azara (Red Wheel/ Weiser, 2002)

Spiritual Doodles & Mental Leapfrogs: A Playbook for Unleashing Spiritual Self-Expression by Katherine Q. Revoir (Red Wheel/Weiser, 2002)

Windows into the Soul: Art as Spiritual Expression by Michael Sullivan (Morehouse Publishing, 2006)

Creativity

The Artist Inside: A Spiritual Guide to Cultivating Your Creative Self by Tom Crockett (Broadway Books, 2000)

The Creative Habit: Learn It and Use It for Life by Twyla Tharp (Simon & Schuster, 2003)

Creative Is a Verb: If You're Alive, You're Creative by Patti Digh (Skirt!, 2010)

Creativity: Where the Divine and the Human Meet by Matthew Fox (Tarcher/Penguin, 2004)

Freeing the Creative Spirit: Drawing on the Power of Art to Tap the Magic and Wisdom Within by Adriana Diaz (HarperSanFrancisco, 1992)

Learning by Heart: Teachings to Free the Creative Spirit by Corita Kent and Jan Steward (Bantam Books, 1992)

The Nine Muses: A Mythological Path to Creativity by Angeles Arrien (Tarcher/Penguin, 2000)

The Soul of Creativity: Insights into the Creative Process edited by Tona Pearce Myers (New World Library, 1999)

Soul Fire: Accessing Your Creativity by Thomas Ryan (Skylight Paths, 2008)

Stoking the Creative Fires: 9 Ways to Rekindle Passion and Imagination by Phil Cousineau (Conari Press, 2008)

Trust the Process: An Artist's Guide to Letting Go by Shaun McNiff (Shambala, 1998)

A Year of Creativity: A Seasonal Guide to New Awareness by Brenda Mallon (Andrews McMeel Publishing, 2002)

General Interest

Art and Soul: 156 Ways to Free Your Creative Spirit by Pam Grout (Andrews McMeel Publishing, 2000)

The Complete Artist's Way: Creativity as a Spiritual Practice by Julia Cameron (Tarcher/Penguin, 2007)

The Creative Call: An Artist's Response to the Way of the Spirit by Janice Elsheimer (Shaw Books, 2001)

Creative Spirituality: The Way of the Artist by Robert Wuthnow (University of California Press, 2003)

Everyday Spiritual Practice: Simple Pathways for Enriching Your Life edited by Scott W. Alexander (Skinner House Books, 2001)

Illuminations: Expressions of the Personal Spiritual Experience edited by Mark L. Tompkins and Jennifer McMahon (Celestial Arts, 2006)

The Way We Pray: Prayer Practices from Around the World by Maggie Oman Shannon (Conari Press, 2001)

Healing/Therapeutic Applications

Art Saves: Stories, Inspiration, and Prompts Sharing the Power of Art by Jenny Doh (North Light Books, 2011)

Awakening the Creative Spirit: Bringing the Arts to Spiritual Direction by Christine Valters Paintner and Betsey Beckman (Church Publishing, 2010)

Craft to Heal: Soothing Your Soul with Sewing, Painting, and Other Pastimes by Nancy Monson (Hats Off Books, 2005)

The Creative Connection: Expressive Arts as Healing by Natalie Rogers (Science & Behavior Books, 1993)

Illuminations: The Healing Image by Madeline McMurray (Wingbow Press, 1988)

The Soul's Palette: Drawing on Art's Transformative Powers for Health and Well-Being by Cathy A. Malchiodi (Shambala, 2002)

Spirituality and Art Therapy: Living the Connection edited by Mimi Farrelly-Hansen (Jessica Kingsley Publishers, 2009)

Philosophy/Culture

Centering: In Pottery, Poetry, and the Person by M. C. Richards (Wesleyan University Press, 1976)

Concerning the Spiritual in Art by Wassily Kandinsky (Dover Publications, Inc., 1977)

The Courage to Create by Rollo May (Bantam Books, 1978)

Craft Activism: People, Ideas, and Projects from the New Community of Handmade and How You Can Join In by Joan Tapper (Potter Craft, 2011)

The Creative Life: 7 Keys to Your Inner Genius by Eric Butterworth (Tarcher/Putnam, 2003)

Desire to Inspire: Using Creative Passion to Transform the World by Christine Mason Miller (North Light Books, 2012)

Image and Spirit: Finding Meaning in Visual Art by Karen Stone (Augsburg Books, 2003)

Making Is Connecting: The Social Meaning of Creativity, From DIY and Knitting to YouTube and Web 2.0 by David Gauntlett (Polity Press, 2011)

The Spirituality of Art by Lois Huey-Heck and Jim Kalnin (Northstone Publishing, 2006)

Walking on Water: Reflections on Faith and Art by Madeleine L'Engle (Harold Shaw Publishers, 1980)

A Way of Working: The Spiritual Dimension of Craft edited by D. M. Dooling (Parabola Books, 1985)

The Zen of Creativity: Cultivating Your Artistic Life by John Daido Loori (Ballantine Books, 2005)

Technique/How-To

Collage for the Soul: Expressing Hopes and Dreams Through Art by Holly Harrison & Paula Grasdal (Quarry Books, 2003)

The Knitting Sutra: Craft as a Spiritual Practice by Susan Gordon Lydon (HarperSanFrancisco, 1997)

Making Crosses: A Creative Connection to God by Ellen Morris Prewitt (Paraclete Press, 2009)

Praying in Color: Drawing a New Path to God by Sybil MacBeth (Paraclete Press, 2007)

Spirit Crafts by Cheryl Owen (CLB International, 1997)

Skylight Paths has done a wonderful job of producing books focusing on particular crafts as spiritual practices. Those books include:

Beading—The Creative Spirit: Finding Your Sacred Center Through the Art of Beadwork by Rev. Wendy Ellsworth (Skylight Paths, 2009)

Contemplative Crochet: A Hands-On Guide for Interlocking Faith and Craft by Cindy Crandall-Frazier (Skylight Paths, 2008)

The Knitting Way: A Guide to Spiritual Self-Discovery by Linda Skolnik and Janice MacDaniels (Skylight Paths, 2005)

The Painting Path: Embodying Spiritual Discovery Through Yoga, Brush and Color by Linda Novick (Skylight Paths, 2007)

The Quilting Path: A Guide to Spiritual Discovery through Fabric, Thread, and Kabbalah by Louise Silk (Skylight Paths, 2006)

The Soulwork of Clay: A Hands-on Approach to Spirituality by Marjory Zoet Bankson (Skylight Paths, 2008)

Interview Subjects

LISA SONORA BEAM is an American visual artist, writer, and global traveler, passionate about the healing and transformative powers of creative expression. She is the author of *The Creative Entrepreneur*, the award-winning and best-selling book on creativity and business. Lisa makes her home south of the border in Oaxaca, Mexico. You can contact Lisa through her websites, lisasonora.com and thecreativeentrepreneur.biz.

RUAH BULL is a spiritual director in private practice in Petaluma, California, and the director of the Contemplative Life Program at The Journey Center in Santa Rosa, California. A trainer for Contemplative Outreach, she teaches centering prayer, a contemporary form of Christian contemplative prayer. Ruah is the coauthor, with Joni Keim, of three classic books in subtle, or spiritual, aromatherapy: *Aromatherapy and Subtle Energy Techniques*, *Aromatherapy Anointing Oils*, and *Daily Aromatherapy,* published by North Atlantic Books. Ruah specializes in supporting people who are being called to the contemplative journey. You can reach her at her website capaxdei-pax.com and at rbcapaxdei@gmail.com.

MARIANNE HIEB, RSM, MFA, ATR, D. Min., directs the Wellness Spirituality Program at Lourdes Wellness Center in Collingswood, New Jersey. She is an artist, art therapist, retreat and spiritual director, and the author of *Inner Journeying Through Art-Journaling*. E-mail her at hiebm@lourdesnet.org, or contact her through lourdeswellnesscenter.org.

SHILOH SOPHIA MCCLOUD is an artist, author, teacher, entrepreneur, and publisher. Her original paintings are internationally collected; she has also published over seven books as well as creativity journals, visionary cards, and offerings of her writings. Shiloh is the founder of Cosmic Cowgirls, a member-run woman- and girl-owned university and publishing house. To learn more about and to contact Shiloh, visit shilohsophiastudios.com.

FRANK MENUSAN is a retired special-education teacher living in Manhattan. Of Muskogee (Creek) heritage, Frank is an acclaimed musician, flute maker, artist, storyteller, and lecturer, and is writing a book on the wisdom ways of his ancestors. To contact Frank, visit frankmenusan.blogspot.com.

REV. JUDITH PRUESS-MELLOW worked for twenty-four years in education and business before going into the ministry. A resident of California, she spent ten years as Minister of Visitation at Los Altos United Methodist Church, then became Executive Director of Senior New Ways, an organization devoted to classes helping seniors live life fully. Now co-owner of Gold Country Seniors Alive, she is also a part-time hospice chaplain. Throughout her ministry spanning eighteen years, she has seen the great value of prayer pockets and prayer shawls in comforting and healing people.

MARY ANNE RADMACHER, who lives in Freeland, Washington, finds that her work circles the globe in many ways—on people's walls at home, work, and school, on their bookshelves, quoted in speeches and reports, and in other books. Her work is included in the *Oxford Dictionary of American Quotations*. Among her accomplishments she happily cites inspiring children to write and has had the opportunity to watch them pursue the process into adulthood. To learn about Mary Anne and to contact her, visit maryanneradmacher.net.

REGINA ROMAN is the director of Sapira—Journey with Purpose, an organization specializing in pilgrimage and study programs in New Mexico, Ireland, and Egypt. She is a practicing spiritual director and a shamanic practitioner in the ancient healing ways. She has presented at international conferences on spiritual practices as well as been published in professional journals. Regina is coauthor of *Journey with Purpose, A Guided Journal to Discover Your Way*, and *Bread Blessing*. A resident of Alexandria, Virginia, she can be contacted at rgroman@comcast.net.

Contributors

PARDIS AMIRSHAHI was the founder and editor of *Living Crafts* magazine, which is now a blog. She loves sewing, knitting, and painting. She lives in Southern California with her husband and daughter. You can reach her at editor@livingcrafts.com.

MARY ANN BRUSSAT is an interfaith minister and the co-director with her husband Frederic of SpiritualityandPractice.com, a multifaith website that provides resources for people on spiritual journeys. She and Frederic are the authors of *Spiritual Literacy: Reading the Sacred in Everyday Life*, a collection of 650 readings on everyday spirituality, and *Spiritual Rx: Prescriptions for Living a Spiritual Life*, on thirty-seven essential practices of the world's religions. She can be reached at Brussat@spiritualityandpractice.com.

TARA CONNOR is a writer who lives in Maine with her husband and two children. She knits, gardens, reads, cooks, and dabbles in genealogical research. And she writes about all of it at Got It, Ma! (gotitma.blogspot.com). She is currently at work on her first novel, the proceeds from which she has already spent on yarn.

FRANNE KETOFSKY EHRLICH DEMETRICIAN was ordained as an interfaith-interspiritual minister in 2003. She has been a holistic massage therapist and Reiki practitioner since 1997 and has been a dean of first-year students at One Spirit Interfaith Seminary in New York City since 2004. She is an artist and a budding professional photographer. Franne lives in Franklin Park, New Jersey, with her beloved husband and best friend, Bob, and their puppy, Sophie.

KAY SAWYER ELLIOTT is a graduate of Liberty University and feels blessed to be the wife of an Air Force chaplain and the mother of four beautiful young women. Kay writes, "I have chosen to be a full-time homemaker which has given me a lot of opportunities to incorporate creativity and art into my daily life. Collage is my favorite form of artistic expression, as I love the immense amount of visual representations I can use to convey a theme or to capture a specific feeling. I am devoted to helping others come to a realization of who they truly are and what specific gifts God has given them. Art brings healing to my soul and a voice to my inner emotions." Contact Kay through her blog TheEtherealArtist. blogspot.com or e-mail her at TheEtherealArtist@gmail.com.

ANN KEELER EVANS, M.DIV., is the minister of the Unitarian Universalist Congregation of the Susquehanna Valley in Pennsylvania. Writer, ritual-maker, speaker, visionary, Ann works to help people ground their personal well-being in healthy community. Find her at annkeelerevans.org or SacredVillage.org.

MONIQUE FELIX was born in Trinidad and is a committed church volunteer and prayer warrior living in San Francisco, California. She does not have an e-mail account or Internet access but stays current with world events so that she can continually "pray the news."

AIMEE GOLANT was voted Best Jewish Artisan Craftsperson in San Francisco, 2010 & 2011, by the readers of the *J. Jewish News Weekly*. Some of Aimee's notable artistic projects include creating the crown for the Women's Torah Project, creating mezuzot for two Space Shuttle missions, and for the National Museum of American Jewish History in Philadelphia. Her art has helped raise money for such charitable organizations as Hadassah and Shalom Bayit. She founded the Metal Art program at the San Francisco Waldorf High School in 2005, where she still teaches classical metalsmithing. She also teaches metal craft at The Crucible in Oakland, California, and at San Francisco's Scintillant Studio. Aimee lives in San Francisco with her husband and son. Visit Aimee at her website, aimeegolant.com.

DEDE NEILSON HELMSWORTH has had many different jobs, from working at an investment banking firm to being a caregiver. Now, she says, she makes things: "I make quilts for AIDS orphans in Africa. I make flannel pajama pants for people I love. I make vegetables in my garden for my family and friends and a food bank. I make food for people who can't make food for themselves. I make socks and sweaters and other cozy things for people I know as well as for people I don't know. I make connections to make a community. I am a wife and a mother and a very grateful person."

CLAIRE JAGEMANN spent over twenty-five years working in public health and social work to stem the HIV/AIDS pandemic in New York and in several countries in Africa. She also spent many years in the theater on stage, in film, and doing commercials and voice-over work. Claire is a Licensed Unity Teacher and an ordained interfaith minister who provides individual grief counseling and conducts many support groups and workshops, including "The Path of Healing," for people who are mourning the loss of a loved one.

DAVID JOHNSON—a self-proclaimed "web guy"—lives in Royal Oak, Michigan, where he produces web applications and sites. He also has been a managing editor in print publishing and a therapist, and recently edited and produced a book on loss and grief with John Schneider, *Finding My Way.* With two master's degrees (one in higher-education administration and one in social work), Dave has worked in a wide range of organizations, and loves to play his guitar in front of audiences.

BRENDA KNIGHT considers herself more of a gardener than a crafter despite winning top prizes for her crewel embroidery as a teen. Brenda is a writer, authoring the American Book Award-winning *Women of the Beat Generation, Rituals for Life,* and *Wild Women and Books.* Brenda volunteers for the American Cancer Society as a counselor for the newly diagnosed and leads writing workshops called "Putting Your Passion on Paper." Founding editor of Viva Editions, a division of Cleis Press, Brenda lives in the San Francisco Bay Area.

SHERRYE THREADGILL MACHA lives in San Antonio, Texas; she has two adult children and has been a kindergarten teacher for twenty-four years. Sherrye is a founding member of the Board of Directors of the San Antonio Children's Museum, as well as a founding member of Positive Pens (a writing group dedicated to writing stories about women affected and infected by HIV) and PEERS for Women (a support group for women affected and infected by HIV). In addition to loving to knit and do needlepoint, she is an avid birder and loves to cook.

BLOSSOM MERZ, also known as "The Weaving Monk," weaves cloth as part of a small spiritual community in southern Oregon. He uses his craft to further their vision of a world where people are more connected to each other and the items in their lives. Blossom and his weaving community sell their wares at events up and down the West Coast as well as through his Etsy.com store. To contact Blossom, visit his website at blossommerz.com.

ANGELA MOBLEY grew up in Altus, Oklahoma. She has lived and studied in Dallas, Texas; Rome, Italy; and Zacatecas, Mexico. She received an M.A. in Painting from Illinois State University in 2003 and an M.F.A. in Film, Video, and New Media from The School of the Art Institute of Chicago in 2005. She currently lives, teaches, and makes her work in Chicago, Illinois. Visit her at angelamobley.com.

AFSANEH NOORI is a change thriver, teacher, author, mentor, speaker, artist, and photographer. Afsaneh's vision and work includes guiding women to not only survive but to embrace and thrive through life's changes; her book *Change Thrivers—Your Resource Guide for Making Change Work* helps the readers become change-ready. Find her on Facebook at the "Art by Afsaneh" page or visit her website at speakerafsanehnoori.com.

ALAN NORDSTROM is a professor of English at Rollins College, where he has taught since 1969. Many of his verses and short essays from the last five years may be read on his blog at alan-nordstrom.blogspot.com.

ZIEK PATERNITI is a licensed massage therapist of twenty-seven years, a self-educated expert on nutrition and autism, and an ordained interfaith minister. She is a self-trained collage and fiber artist, who teaches classes in expressing one's deeper self through altered books, art journals, and other creative adventures. She lives in New York with her husband Tony and her daughter, Elena, who gives new and majestic meaning to the so-called low-end of the autism spectrum. Ziek finds her greatest inspiration from the life and teachings of Avatar Meher Baba.

VLADIMIR SANCHEZ was born in Chile. He studied Systems Engineering at the Universidad Catolica de Valparaiso, where he met his future wife, an American, who was spending a year abroad in Chile. After marrying in Chile and having a child, they moved to the United States in 2005 to start a new life in San Francisco. Vlad works as an IT consultant for well-known companies, and can be reached at blasbox-crafts@yahoo.com.

ELKA EASTLY VERA, M.A., is an author, artist, and transformative coach whose mission is to help people cultivate their connection with the Divine. She is the creator of *Seeds of Wisdom* oracle and guidebook. Discover more at ElkaVera.com.

Acknowledgments

WHILE WORKING ON THIS PROJECT, I HAVE BEEN MOVED AND touched by many, many expressions of the greatest generosity there is: generosity of spirit. From the interview subjects and contributors who so graciously shared their thoughts and insights, to the very real sacrifices made by my husband and daughter to give me the space and time to write this book, this project—and I, through it—was blessed.

So let me name just a few of my blessings: Thank you to Brenda Knight, the common denominator behind all my books, for her wonderful guidance and enthusiastic support; Krishna Bhat for his wonderful illustrations; and to all the talented people at Viva Editions who helped to bring *Crafting Calm* into form.

Deep and heartfelt thanks to everyone who contributed to this book with suggestions or actual contributions, including Pardis Amirshahi, Peace Arnold, Mary Ann Brussat, Tara Conner, Jo Crawford, Tom Cumminsky, Bob and Franne Demetrician, Kay Sawyer Elliott, Ann Keeler Evans, Monique Felix, Aimee Golant, Dede Neilson Helmsworth, Claire Jagemann, Dave Johnson, Sherrye Threadgill Macha, Lauren McLaughlin, Blossom Merz, Angela Mobley, Afsaneh Noori, Alan Nordstrom, Ziek Paterniti, Vladimir Sanchez, and Elka Eastly Vera.

Special thanks to those who so generously shared their crafting and spiritual practices in lengthy interviews: Lisa Sonora Beam, Ruah Bull, Marianne Hieb, Shiloh Sophia McCloud, Frank Menusan, Judith Pruess-Mellow, Mary Anne Radmacher, and Regina Roman.

Deep thanks to Mary Anne Radmacher, for her tangible and intangible gifts and for the foreword to this book, which was a blessing to me (and whose writing and artwork is a blessing to all of us); and to my spiritual directors, Janice Farrell (whose influence I mention in the introduction to this book) and Catherine Regan, who have been cherished sources of support and insight through the years.

As always, I am so grateful for all of the wonderful people in my treasured network of colleagues, church members, friends, and family members—and I am especially grateful for my beautiful family; my husband, Scott Shannon, and my daughter, Chloe Shannon.

Given the support, visible and Invisible, that has surrounded this project, I can't help but be reminded of the words of Matthew Fox: "To create is to share. To share is to give back gift for gift, blessing for blessing." I am so grateful for these gifts, these blessings, and can only pray that this book might bless others as I have been blessed. Thank you, God.

About the Author

REV. MAGGIE OMAN SHANNON, M. A., IS AN INTERFAITH minister, spiritual director, workshop and retreat facilitator, and author of five previous books: *Prayers for Healing*; *The Way We Pray: Prayer Practices from Around the World*; *A String and a Prayer: How to Make and Use Prayer Beads* (coauthor); *One God, Shared Hope*; and *Prayers for Hope and Comfort*. In 2000, Oman Shannon founded The New Story, a coaching and consulting business focused on helping people create deeper meaning in their lives.

The former editor of three national magazines, including *The Saturday Evening Post*, Oman Shannon also served as Director of Marketing for the Institute of Noetic Sciences. Her writing has appeared in publications including *Utne Reader* and Beliefnet.com; and her work has been featured in publications ranging from the *Miami Herald* to *Spirituality and Health* magazine. She has taught workshops at venues including California Pacific Medical Center's Institute for Health and Healing and Chautauqua Institution in Chautauqua, New York.

In addition to being a certified life coach, Oman Shannon completed the three-year training program of the Spiritual Directors Institute at Mercy Center in Burlingame, California. A graduate of Smith College, Oman Shannon also holds an M.A. degree in Culture and Spirituality from Holy Names University. She is an ordained interfaith minister who graduated from Manhattan's One Spirit Interfaith Seminary in 2010.

Oman Shannon currently has the honor of serving as Spiritual Director of Unity Spiritual Center of San Francisco. She lives in San Francisco with her husband and nine-year-old daughter who also loves to "do crafts." She can be reached through her website, www.maggieomanshannon.com.

Index

To Our Readers

Viva Editions publishes books that inform, enlighten, and entertain. We do our best to bring you, the reader, quality books that celebrate life, inspire the mind, revive the spirit, and enhance lives all around. Our authors are practical visionaries: people who offer deep wisdom in a hopeful and helpful manner. Viva was launched with an attitude of growth and we want to spread our joy and offer our support and advice where we can to help you live the Viva way: vivaciously!

We're grateful for all our readers and want to keep bringing you books for inspired living. We invite you to write to us with your comments and suggestions, and what you'd like to see more of. You can also sign up for our online newsletter to learn about new titles, author events, and special offers.

Viva Editions
2246 Sixth St.
Berkeley, CA 94710
www.vivaeditions.com
(800) 780-2279
Follow us on Twitter @vivaeditions
Friend/fan us on Facebook